To Charles Schwartz

in token of your Confirmation

March 25th, 1934.

Rev. W. L. Weber.

Revelations 2:10.

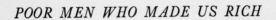

POOR MEN WHO MADE US RICH

Other Books by
Archer Wallace

✳

Adventures in the Air
Men Who Played the Game
Mothers of Famous Men
Hands Around the World
More Stories of Grit
Boys Who Made Good
Heroes of Peace
Blazing New Trails
Stories of Grit
Overcoming Handicaps

✳

POOR MEN WHO MADE US RICH

by
ARCHER WALLACE

Illustrations by
NORMAN DEER

HARPER & BROTHERS
Publishers
NEW YORK AND LONDON
1933

CONTENTS

ILLUSTRATIONS

INTRODUCTION

THERE are people who think of a successful man as one who has become rich; the richer he is the greater is his success. This is a false standard. Many so-called successful men have been utterly selfish and failed as men. On the other hand, there have been men, in every country and in every age, who thought of others rather than of themselves and who were rich only in kindness and sympathy and good-will. Some of these men often lacked the bare necessities of life and not a few died in abject poverty. This book tells of fourteen such men whose names are held in everlasting remembrance.

Toronto   ARCHER WALLACE

POOR MEN WHO MADE US RICH

SOCRATES

IN THE fifth century B.C. the city of Athens was at the height of its glory. Her sculptors, artists, poets, and philosophers were making the city famous for its culture—so famous that after twenty-five centuries the mere mention of Athens suggests wisdom and beauty. In those far-off days there were no schools anywhere to compare with the ones at Athens.

Among those who moved along its streets was a strange figure, one whose appearance and manner of living were in striking contrast to the life around him. This man was Socrates. He was born at Athens in 470 B.C., the son of a stone-mason, a trade at which he worked himself for some time. The Greeks worshiped beauty, as no other people have ever done, yet Socrates is said to have been far from beautiful; most historians say he was ugly.

There is a sculptored head of him in the British Museum, and it would certainly seem as if he were far from handsome. His head was square, his features flat and irregular, eyes small and peering, and his whole appearance almost grotesque. Yet of all the men who then lived in

Athens, none are remembered with anything like the affection and esteem that men have for Socrates.

He cared little or nothing for most of the things upon which men set their affection; wealth, fame, and worldly honor did not interest him. He lived simply and wore shabby clothes. The same coat served him in summer and winter. He walked along the streets in bare feet. When urged to increase his income, he said he would adjust his needs to his income, no matter how small it might be.

Although he lived in an age when men considered it manly to strike blow for blow and to repay insult with savage retaliation, he repaid evil with good, and cast all bitterness, hatred, and malice out of his heart. He spoke fearlessly against the evils of his day, even when he knew that some men of influence and power would never forgive him for doing so. When he faced men who held his life in their hands, he was as calm and unruffled as the sea on a calm day.

At the market place and the forum in Athens there were a great many talkers. These men, now called Sophists, had gained a reputation for wisdom they did not deserve. Their talk was idle and meaningless. Wherever Socrates saw a group he joined it and began asking questions. His search was for truth and he showed how

SOCRATES

many of the beliefs of his day were mere superstitions.

He would talk with anyone who was sincere. He had one object, and only one, in all his conversation—to find out the truth, to reveal the folly of idle superstition and the wickedness of falsehood. He believed that if men knew the truth they would obey it. He said that he heard a voice within his soul urging him on, and he felt sure it was the voice of God.

Although many ridiculed Socrates, and others hated him, the sheer force of his strong and pure personality began to tell and the young men of Athens especially felt the spell of his teaching and life. They were thrilled by his appeals for heroic and virtuous living and he never lacked hearers. "Gradually their interest was aroused, their attention grew fixed, and then their hearts beat faster, their eyes swam with tears, their very souls were touched and thrilled by the voice of the charmer." It was a period of change in Athens. For generations Athenians had accepted as true the legends and myths which told about the strange doings of their gods.

Thoughtful people found it difficult to believe these myths. Socrates seems to have believed in the gods as all men did at that time, but he regarded many of the stories as superstitions. "He believed in the God of all mankind, the Creator of the universe. He believed in prayer, but he refused to pray for what he wanted, but prayed that God would give him what was best. There is a beautiful picture of an afternoon he spent sitting in the sun with his friend Phædrus. As the sun went down they rose to go, but first Socrates offered a prayer to whatever powers were guarding the charming spot where they had rested. This was the prayer that came from his heart: 'O beloved Pan, and all ye gods whose dwelling is in this place, grant me to be beautiful in soul, and all that I possess of outward things to be at peace with them within. Teach me to think wisdom the only riches, and give me so much wealth, and so much only, as a good and holy man could manage or enjoy.' "

Some one has said that all men recognize God's voice when they hear it speaking through other men. That certainly was true in the case of Socrates. Many unlikely men were attracted to him. Among them was the dashing soldier and commander, Alcibiades. Citizens of Athens greatly admired this fearless soldier, but his gay and dissolute life was the talk of the city. Yet Alcibiades felt himself strangely drawn to the philosopher whose life was such a contrast with his own. In a study of Socrates, the English journalist, Mr. Arthur Mee, writes:

"A strange sight it was to see these ill-matched men—Alcibiades, the handsome good-for-nothing, and ugly Socrates in his shabby coat. But that magic power of Socrates drew all men unto him. 'When I listen to him,' said Alcibiades, 'my heart beats with excitement. He has only to speak and the tears flow. Pericles never moved me in this way, but he makes me think that life is not worth living so long as I am what I am. So there is nothing for me to do but to stop my ears against this siren's song and to fly for my life, that I may not grow old sitting at his feet. No one would think that I had any shame, but I am ashamed in the presence of Socrates.' "

It was not to be expected that one as fearless and outspoken against evil as Socrates would be left unmolested. As five centuries later the Jewish leaders were stirred up to hatred by the life and teaching of Jesus, so in Athens first the ruling classes and later the common people became angered at the man whose questions they could not answer and whose life was a reproach to them. The friends of Socrates wished him to modify his speech so as not to offend the rulers, but he made no compromise with evil or with superstition.

Then there came a day when this notice was posted in Athens: "Socrates is guilty of crime; first, for not worshipping the gods whom the city worships, but introducing new divinities of his own; secondly, for corrupting the youth. The penalty due is death."

Consternation reigned in Athens that day. Socrates was over seventy years of age. For fifty years he had been prominent in that city of great men. No one could point to an evil thing he had done. His whole life had been that of an earnest and kind seeker after truth. Athens had never known a purer soul. But he need not die, he was offered freedom if he would promise to stop teaching. He refused. He faced trial before five hundred and fifty-seven of his fellow citizens.

Socrates spoke in his own behalf in eloquent speech. His speech was not only a defense, but also a lecture. There was not one apologetic note in that address. If the jurymen expected him to cringe and plead for his life, they were disappointed. He would not accept acquittal, he told them, if it were granted on the ground that he cease teaching.

By a narrow majority—only five or six—Socrates was found guilty. According to custom, he was asked to say what punishment he would consider just. He faces them again; no longer a free man but condemned, with sentence of death very near. Fearlessly he replies that he thinks he should be recognized as a public benefactor and given a pension for life; but as an alternative he proposes a small fine. The court rejected his proposal with scorn. *He was condemned to death.*

He took his sentence. They would gain little by the condemnation, he told the judges in a farewell speech which will never be forgotten. He was far advanced in years, and in a very few years would have died a natural death. He said:

"O Judges, be of good cheer about death and know of a certainty that no evil can happen to a good man, either in life or after. I am not angry with my accusers, or with you, my condemners. The hour of departing is at hand, and we go our ways, I to die, and you to live. Which is better, God alone knows."

His death was delayed by a curious circumstance. A sacred vessel had been sent to the festival of Delos. It was a law that no execution could take place while this ship was away, and so for thirty days Socrates lived in prison, with fetters on his ankles and surrounded by his friends. Among this group was young Plato, who left an account of the sayings of Socrates—sayings so calm and brave—that forever stamp this Athenian teacher as one of the purest and noblest men that ever lived.

Crito, a friend, tried to induce Socrates to escape. Friends, well furnished with money, were waiting, the jailer could be bribed, all had been arranged. Socrates refused to fall in with the plans made by his friends. All his life, he said, he had urged men to obey the law; how could he, through fear of death, break the law?

Then one morning, before dawn, Crito awoke the sleeping Socrates. The sacred vessel returning to Athens had been sighted. Calmly he gave directions regarding the disposal of what little property he had. The next day was his last upon earth. Toward evening, the jailer, in tears, brought him the hemlock, the poison which he was to drink. He held it, then drank it, and began to walk about as the jailer told him to do.

Phædon, who was present, thus describes the scene: "In spite of myself the tears were flowing fast, so that I covered my face, but certainly I was not weeping for him, but at the thought of losing such a companion. I could hardly believe that I was present at the death of a friend, and therefore I did not pity him. His manner and his language were so noble and fearless in the hour of death that he appeared blessed. I thought that in going to the other world he could not be without a divine call, and that he would be happy, if ever man was, when he arrived there."

When the poison worked so that Socrates could no longer walk about, he lay still, awaiting the end. One last question his friends ask of him. What should be done with his body? "You may do with it what you like," whispered the dying man, "provided you do not imagine it to be me."

II

BARUCH SPINOZA

BARUCH SPINOZA was born at Amsterdam on November 24, 1632. In face of bitter persecution in Spain his Jewish parents, together with many of their fellow countrymen, had fled into the Netherlands, where they found refuge. One day his father sent young Spinoza to collect some money from a woman in Amsterdam which she owed him. When he entered her house he found her reading the Bible. She motioned him to sit down until she had finished reading and engaged in prayer. The boy then told her his errand, and the woman counted out the money and gave it to him, at the same time saying she hoped he would never depart from the law of Moses and that he would grow up to be a good man like his father. She wanted to put the money into the bag he carried, but he thought it would be better to count it. When he did so he found she had, by a clever trick, dropped two coins through a slit in the top of the table, hoping thereby to cheat the child. Young Spinoza never forgot that experience, and while throughout his life he remained a

BARUCH SPINOZA

very reverent man, there was nothing he despised so much as hypocrisy.

Spinoza even as a boy was very thoughtful and deeply interested in religious matters. Before he was fifteen years of age he found difficulties in connection with the Scriptures and the Jewish religion which no one seemed able to answer to his satisfaction. A kind and sympathetic teacher could have helped him a great deal, but the rabbis and other leaders of that day were intolerant and bitterly resented the questions he asked.

One by one his Jewish friends fell away from him. They neither liked the questions he asked nor could they answer them. He was seldom seen at the services of the synagogue and soon not at all. The jealousy of the heads of the synagogue was easily roused. Two so-called friends then visited him and asked him to state his position, which he did with the sincerity and frankness of his nature. These men then reported what he had said, probably adding something of their own. False rumors concerning him quickly spread. His enemies were so bitter that they wanted to have him condemned and excommunicated from the synagogue without even giving him a chance. However, at last he was summoned to appear before the authorities.

Feeling that his conscience had nothing with which to reproach him, he went cheerfully to the synagogue and stood before his judges. He was accused of the most awful of all crimes, namely, contempt for the law, and he was given a chance to clear himself of it. He denied this, but when he tried to explain that he thought many things in the Scripture were not meant to be taken in just the way the religious leaders had interpreted them, the judges were greatly angered, and the sentence of excommunication from the synagogue was passed upon him, and carried out on July 27, 1656.

This act on the part of his bigoted judges was a cruel one, for excommunication meant that no Jew must under any circumstances render him service, or he would be visited with the same punishment. Just how bitter the feeling was among Jews to an excommunicated person can be gathered from the following:

"Let him [Spinoza] be accursed by day and accursed by night; let him be accursed in his lying down and accursed in his rising up; accursed in going out and accursed in coming in. May the Lord never more pardon or acknowledge him. May the wrath and displeasure of the Lord burn henceforth against this man: load him with all the curses written in the Book of the Law, and blot out his name from under the sky. May the Lord sever him for evil from all the tribes of Israel, weigh him with all the maledictions of the firmament contained in the Book

of the Law. . . . All persons are admonished
that none must hold converse with Spinoza by
word of mouth nor by writing: no one shall do
him any service; no one shall abide under the
same roof with him; no one shall approach
within four cubits' length of him; and no one
shall read any documents dictated by him or
written by his hand."

Spinoza took this terrible sentence very
calmly. He knew that for the remainder of his
life he would be cut off from his relatives and
former friends, that he would be hated and despised and persecuted by them. Nevertheless, he
retained a calmness of temper and sweetness of
disposition which only served to exasperate
those who hated him. A vicious attack upon his
life was made by a man who tried to murder
him with a dagger. Spinoza then felt that he
should be protected in some way. He found a
home with a learned Dutch physician named
named Francis Van den Ende. This man, who
taught Greek and Latin to a number of pupils
with considerable success, looked after Spinoza,
receiving him into his own house and exacting
no other return than that the young Jew should
sometimes help him to instruct his pupils.

Like every other Jew, Spinoza had learned a
trade, and he had become an expert in the
preparation of lenses for microscopes and tele-
scopes. In this art he excelled so much that there

are still in existence pieces of his handiwork which he did at that time. He was, however, above everything else a philosopher, and so ardent in the search for truth was he that often for months at a time he did not go outside his humble lodgings. He spent his days in such close study that he became one of the most influential philosophers of his day. A number of the younger men in Amsterdam, many of whom were students of medicine or theology, came to regard him as their leader. He did not enjoy controversy for its own sake, but was naturally of a mild and lovable disposition; nevertheless, he was always eager to assist those who, like himself, were seekers after truth.

An investigation of his affairs at this time shows that he lived on a few cents a day. His wants were few, and for the luxuries of life he had no desire whatever. There have been few men who cared less for money. One of his intimate friends, named Simon de Vries, wanted to make him a present of one thousand dollars. Spinoza politely declined to take any of it. He said: "Nature is content with little, and when she is satisfied, so am I." Shortly after, when this man lay dying, having neither wife nor children, he wanted to leave all he had to Spinoza, for he was bitterly estranged from his brother. Spinoza, however, pleaded with him not to do this, and at last succeeded in getting him to leave his fortune to his brother. The clause in the will stipulated that Spinoza must have an annual pension of two hundred and fifty dollars. This he refused to take, but finally was induced to allow a grant of one hundred and fifty dollars to be paid to him annually.

How little Spinoza cared for money was made clear when King Louis XIV offered him a substantial pension on condition that Spinoza should dedicate his next book to him. This Spinoza courteously but firmly declined to do. Some years later he was offered a position as professor of philosophy at the University of Heidelberg. This offer was couched in the most complimentary terms, the only condition laid down being that he would not teach anything that called in question the established religion of the state. Spinoza felt that he could not honestly comply with this condition. Devout man though he was, he knew there were many things about the established religion with which he could not agree, and he could not reconcile himself to accept the position. He preferred to have his freedom and live on a few coppers daily.

He believed that all the vices of men were due to ignorance, and he felt sure that if they could be shown the right way, they would follow it. Even the people who hounded him and never ceased to spread evil and lying rumors about him never caused him to be angry in return. With tireless patience and long suffering he tried to show them what he thought was the truth. He was never known to show any bitter resentment against those who had so grievously injured him.

Although after his excommunication from the synagogue he did not join any other religious sect, he lived with a family of devout Lutherans, and he was deeply impressed by their simple piety and earnest faith. Frequently he attended their church, and never ceased to express appreciation of all he saw and heard. Often in the street he would take the trouble to tell people about the excellent sermon he had heard from the pastor of the Lutheran church.

In spite of his poverty he was as generous as his small income would permit. Often when in extreme need himself he would lend or give away that which meant he would have to go hungry or reduce his daily fare. He did not at any time in his life enjoy good health, and the manner of his life probably hastened his end. Gradually tuberculosis laid its dread hand upon him and he slowly wasted away. The end came when he died peacefully at Amsterdam on February 21, 1677, being just a little over forty-four years of age.

At his own express wish his chief books were not published until after his death, and even then, such was his humility, that he wished they might be published without his name attached. He was willing to be completely forgotten if only the cause of truth should be advanced. There have been few men who lived a more simple, kindly, and blameless life than Baruch Spinoza. A sentence contained in one of his books sums up exactly what he wished for mankind. He said, "The greatest treasure in the world is not that which for one to possess the rest must lose, but where all can possess alike; and where one man's wealth promotes his neighbor's."

III

JOHN MILTON

JOHN MILTON, the great English poet, was born in Bread Street, London, on December 9, 1608, just eight years before Shakespeare died. It is quite possible that when he was a boy Milton saw Shakespeare. His father was a man of much influence who had been educated at the University of Oxford, but later was disinherited because he embraced Protestantism. John Milton himself began to study so early that by the time he was twelve he was much ahead of boys several years his senior. He studied almost continuously in spite of headaches and weak eyes. During these days he so impaired his eyesight that it never recovered. There were no public schools in those days in the sense that we have them now, and a great deal depended upon parents. John Milton was fortunate in having a father who was anxious to see him well educated. He wrote, "My father caused me to be instructed daily both at the grammar school and by bringing teachers into our home."

At the age of sixteen Milton entered Christ's College, Cambridge, where he remained for

seven years and five months. Here his record
was exceptionally brilliant, although, when he
first entered college his handsome appearance
earned for him the nickname "The Lady of
Christ's College." This seems to have been due
not only to the charm of his personal appearance, but also to the fact that his strict regard
for morals annoyed rougher and coarser students. While at college Milton's poetic genius
first began to manifest itself, and he wrote many
poems of great beauty. Although he had gone
to Cambridge with the intention of becoming a
clergyman, he soon abandoned that idea and
turned to a life of literature and poetry. His
father agreed to this, and seems to have been in
a position to help his son considerably. For several years following the completion of his college course he continued to turn out poetry of
such a high order that friends agreed he was
following the natural course in becoming a poet.

A poem entitled "Ode on the Morning of
Christ's Nativity" first turned men's attention
to him. Other poems which soon followed established his reputation as one of the nation's leading poets. In 1638, just after he had passed his
thirtieth birthday, John Milton left England
for a tour of the Continent, something which in
those days was a much more serious undertaking
than it is today. He wandered in sunny Italy,

JOHN MILTON

enchanted as he walked through countrysides where Dante, Petrarch, and others had lived and died.

In the city of Florence he was made much of by the citizens, who recognized the strength and beauty of his poems which he read to them from time to time. From Florence he went to Rome, and spent several months there visiting the ruins of that great historic city and the art galleries until his lively imagination was kindled amid such classic surroundings. Later he visited Geneva in Switzerland, which was the centre of Protestant influence and learning. This visit was a very important one, for there he came in contact with great men of such strong religious convictions that the stamp of their influence remained with him for the rest of his life. He returned to England in August, 1639, after an absence from his native land of fifteen months.

The cause of his return was that the discontent in England in the time of King Charles I had reached such a point that it was evident civil war was impending. Milton threw in his lot with the Puritans, and by constant and fearless use of his vigorous pen soon became one of the leading figures in these eventful days in English history. King Charles I was beheaded by an indignant people in 1649, and one of the

first men to attach himself openly to the new
Republic was John Milton. This he did by pub-
lication of a pamphlet in which he defended the
action of those who had beheaded the king.
Naturally the chiefs of the new Republic saw
the importance of securing the services of so
able and distinguished a man as Milton, and in
March, 1649, he was offered, and accepted, the
secretaryship for foreign towns of the new Commonwealth.

This important position John Milton held for
nearly ten years. He must have seen a great deal
of Oliver Cromwell, and from time to time he
referred to Cromwell as one of the greatest and
best men of his generation or of many generations. He was unstinted in praise whenever re-
ferring to the great Commoner, although,
unfortunately, we have no record of how Cromwell regarded Milton. During these years Milton's pen was never idle. Those who sympa-
thized with the cause of the Stuart kings were
active on the Continent in discrediting the Puritans. Milton was just as active in the defence,
and wrote a series of crushing pamphlets in answer to those who he felt were misrepresenting
the leaders of the Puritan movement in England.

Milton had married in the summer of 1643.
By his marriage he had three daughters, Anne,

Mary, and Deborah. There was also a boy who died when eight years of age. In 1651, when he was forty-three years of age, right in the prime of his energetic manhood, John Milton lost his eyesight, and for the remainder of his life was absolutely dependent upon his friends. He continued to perform his official duties, and for a while hoped that Thevenot, an eminent French oculist, might restore his eyesight. In this he was bitterly disappointed, and there are few passages in all literature more thrilling than those in which this valiant heart accepted his fate. Before the final interview with Thevenot, he wrote:

"Whatever ray of hope there may be for me from the famous physician, I prepare and compose myself accordingly. My frequent thought is that since many days of darkness are destined for everyone, my darkness, by the singular kindness of God, will be amid rest and studies, and the voices and greetings of my friends have been much easier to bear because of this. . . . Verily, God looks out for me, and provides for me, leading me forth with His hand through my whole life. I shall willingly, if it be His will, give my eyes their long holiday."

After he knew that there was no hope whatever, and that blindness would be his lot for the remainder of his life, he wrote:

Yet I argue not
  Against heaven's hand or will, nor bate a jot
Of heart or hope, but still bear up, and steer
  Right onward.

The vigour and beauty of Milton's poetry is
all the more wonderful when we remember that
his eyes could no longer see nature, as others
saw it. Nowhere is he more tender or impres-
sive than when he alludes to his blindness. He
is generally thought of as a stern and harsh man,
one who was more admired than loved; but who
could read the following verses without realiz-
ing how solitary the great man was?

  Thus with the year
Seasons return; but not to me returns
  Day, or the sweet approach of even or morn,
Or sight of vernal bloom, or summer's rose,
  Or flocks, or herds, or human face divine;
But cloud instead, and ever-during dark
  Surrounds me, from the cheerful ways of
    men
Cut off; and for the book of knowledge fair,
  Presented with a universal blank
Of Nature's works to me expunged and rased,
  And wisdom at one entrance quite shut out.
So much the rather thou, Celestial Light,
  Shine inward, and the mind through all her
    power.

Irradiate: there plant eyes, all mist from thence
*   Purge and disperse, that I may see and tell*
Of things invisible to mortal sight.

In 1658 Cromwell died, and the enemies of
the Commonwealth began to agitate for the
restoration of the monarchy. At this time, when
such a change seemed inevitable, Milton refused to be silent. He steadfastly opposed the
return of the king's son, but it was in vain. On
May 29, 1660, King Charles II made his tri-
umphal entry into London. The Republicans
scattered themselves to all parts of the country,
and Milton was forced to hide in an obscure
part of the city. How he escaped the scaffold at
that time was a mystery and is still a mystery.
His books were publicly burned, and the appearance of the blind man on the streets himself would surely have meant he would have
been arrested or assaulted by those who had
feared and trembled at his writings. He lived in
a small house near the heart of the city, and
writing of his condition at that time he said:

Though fallen on evil days,
*   On evil days though fallen, and evil tongues,*
In darkness, and with dangers compassed round,
*   And solitude.*

These evil days of which he wrote were those

immediately following the Restoration when Milton was regarded as an outcast, a detested Republican, and one who many doubtless thought ought to die on the scaffold. He left London for a while, but returned after the great fire of 1666, and spent the remainder of his life, eight years in all, in the city. It was during this period that he wrote his great poems "Paradise Lost," "Paradise Regained" and "Samson Agonistes." From the beginning even his severest critics recognized the greatness of these works. A poet of his day said, "This man, Milton, cuts us all out, and the ancients too." With the passing of the years his greatness was recognized, at least to some extent, and visitors of all ranks sought him out for the honour of his society and conversation.

He dictated much of his works to his daughters, who, although they could not understand the languages, learned to read and pronounce Hebrew, Greek, Latin, and French. That they should rebel against this treatment perhaps was natural, but he felt their conduct to be blameworthy. He complained that his daughters not only neglected him, but sold some of his books. It should be remembered, however, that these motherless girls—for their mother died and Milton married again—were ill looked after and poorly educated; their conduct at least can be understood.

Milton's blindness, though it must have been a blow at the time, at least gave him leisure to think in solitude about some great subjects which, had his eyesight remained perfect, he might not have felt he had time to study. While he did not live in direst want, it is evident that during the last fourteen years of his life he knew poverty as well as persecution. He had inherited very little from his father, had failed to get the inheritance from his first wife, had lost almost all the money he had loaned to others, and by an accident his house was burned. It seemed as if one calamity heaped upon another until in obscurity and loneliness he produced his great works. He died on Sunday, November 8, 1674, at the age of sixty-five years and eleven months, and was buried in the Church of St. Giles near by.

It has often been said of him, "His soul was like a star and dwelt apart." Neither loneliness, persecution, poverty nor blindness sufficed to quench the dauntless spirit of this man whose riches were not of this world.

IV

REMBRANDT

REMBRANDT, one of the greatest artists of all time, was born at Leyden in Holland about the year 1606. He was the son of a miller, the fifth in a family of six children. It was his parents' wish that he should become a lawyer, but the boy showed no inclination for it; on the other hand, he was so keenly interested in sketching that his parents allowed him to follow his own bent, and apprenticed him for three years to a painter named Jacob van Swanenburgh.

According to the custom of that day Rembrandt went to live with the artist and his family. Swanenburgh treated the boy kindly; he recognized his remarkable gifts, and prophesied for him a brilliant future. He soon realized that there was little more he could teach him, and in 1624 Rembrandt was sent to Amsterdam to study under Pieter Lastman, a famous painter of his day. Soon afterwards he returned to his father's home in Leyden, where he remained for six years.

Even as a small boy Rembrandt had found hundreds of subjects in his native town he wanted to sketch. Almost everything he looked at suggested a picture. He studied the coming and going of simple, kindly country folk with their wooden shoes; the more ambitious city folk swaggering along with their brilliant scarves and feathered hats; the slowly-moving, heavily-laden barges on the canals; the arrival of travelers in lumbering coaches; and the never-ceasing stream of wretched beggars, many of them crippled and all in rags. Not only in the daytime, but when darkness came he saw pictures everywhere. He watched the expressions on people's faces as they sat in the glow of the flickering firelight—sometimes he laughed aloud at the fantastic shapes he saw in the fire, or started uneasily at the shapes and gloomy shadows thrown by the uncertain light of the candle. In his home there was a large Bible with fine engravings which was a source of never-ending delight to him, and as he listened to his mother telling Bible stories he seemed to see and hear the people of whom she told.

All his life Rembrandt found great delight in portraying Bible scenes. Some of these pictures are among the most famous in the world and are found in great museums in many lands. Among the best known are: "Saint Paul in Prison," "The Supper at Emmaus," "Samson's Capture by the Philistines," "Saint Peter among the Servants of the High Priest," "Christ Disputing with the Doctors in the Temple," "The

REMBRANDT

Good Samaritan," and "The Flight into Egypt."

Rembrandt's affection for his parents led him to make many sketches of them when he was still a boy. There is a lifelike portrait of his father in the Royal Gallery at Cassel, while a drawing of his kindly mother is an exquisite masterpiece—a clever boy's tender tribute to a good mother.

In 1630 Rembrandt left his native town and moved to Amsterdam, where he lived until his death, thirty-nine years later. Many artists have found it necessary to travel a great deal in order to get suggestions for pictures, but Rembrandt was never a traveler; few great men saw less of the world. For three hundred years men have admired the pictures of Rembrandt, yet these masterpieces are almost entirely of people and scenes he saw around him every day.

He studied the faces of people he passed on the street, some lighted up with joy or eagerness, others gloomy with grief or disappointment. He noticed how quickly some changed from calmness to anger and to passion. He looked long and earnestly into the mirror and studied in his own face, laughter, anger, happiness, sorrow, thoughtfulness, and even vacancy. No man ever drew his own likeness so often, and this he did, not from vanity, but because he wanted to study human nature rather than simply follow the style of other painters.

He attempted to sketch whatever came under his notice: peasants buying and selling in the marketplace, merry groups of skaters on the ponds, wandering musicians in the streets, the rat-killer—familiar sight in those days—pancake-women peddling their wares from door to door, and weary beggars limping along the lanes in tattered clothing. Nothing escaped his attention. With a few swift strokes this man of genius could draw a picture that no one could forget.

He was keenly interested in everything around him, and no fewer than five hundred and fifty paintings are attributed to him, besides three hundred and twenty-nine etchings and many drawings. When one remembers the general excellence of his work, that many of his pictures have never been surpassed and seldom equaled, it is astonishing that any man should, in the course of his lifetime, have accomplished so much. His energy was amazing. Soon Rembrandt's fame as a portrait-painter became such that his studio was crowded with would-be sitters. One of his pupils wrote, "When he was painting he would have refused to receive the greatest sovereign on earth, and would have compelled him to wait or call again when he was willing to see him."

At the height of his fame Rembrandt had no serious rival; he was supreme. Distinguished people came, in some instances, hundreds of miles, then waited for weeks, and counted themselves fortunate to have the great artist paint their pictures. For twelve or perhaps fifteen years Rembrandt's popularity lasted, and the portraits he painted during that period are to be found in nearly every famous art gallery to-day. The most famous of all Rembrandt's works is the picture named "The Night Watch," now in the art gallery at Amsterdam. While he was painting it his wife was slowly failing in health, and the year of his greatest triumph was saddened by her death. This was, perhaps, the heaviest of all the shadows which darkened his life, and one from which he never fully recovered.

While he was still in early middle life several crushing blows came to Rembrandt. His first-born child, Rumbartus, died in infancy; another child, a girl, died soon after her baptism. A few years later another little daughter, to whom he was much attached, passed away. A boy, Titus, alone survived, and upon him Rembrandt lavished the affection of his aching heart, and he left dozens of charming sketches of his wife tenderly nursing the child. Titus grew to young manhood, then died, and the great painter was for the remainder of his life a lonely man.

Like so many other men of genius, Rembrandt does not seem to have been able to manage his financial affairs. He was hopelessly extravagant. He had a mania for collecting antiques, and haunted salesrooms until his home was filled with "ancient armor, stuffed birds, paintings, prints, shells, and horns of animals." A great painter of his day says that "he was kind to the point of being foolish," and undoubtedly many took advantage of this strange genius who never seemed to know the value of money.

One of his pupils, Baldinucci, wrote, "When Rembrandt was present at a sale, especially one of paintings or drawings by masters, he would start with so high a bid that no other purchasers would offer, and to persons who expressed surprise at his conduct he would say that in this way he intended to exalt his profession." He either loaned or gave away to fellow artists almost everything he had. In spite of his large earnings he fell into serious financial difficulties, and for the last twenty years of his life was never out of debt.

In 1656 Rembrandt was so seriously involved in debt that his home was taken from him, his possessions sold, and he was declared bankrupt. His popularity had gradually waned. There was also a serious depression in trade, but the chief cause of Rembrandt's misfortunes was his gen-

erosity and extravagance, together with his utter failure to handle money. He never gave any
thought to the future, and so he came to utter
poverty with all its humiliations and misery.

Rembrandt was never a vain man, not even
when royalty waited for his favors. He cared
little or nothing for the polite society of his day.
He was too much absorbed in his work to be
hampered by indulging in social functions. Con-
vention and external restraints were distasteful
to him. He was a man of the people, and his
deep sympathy caused him to love people for
themselves and not for what they had. But when
he was cast into prison for non-payment of his
debts, he was stunned and bewildered. He
bowed under the disgrace, crushed and broken.

During these sorrowful years—these closing
years—of his life, Rembrandt continued to paint
with restless energy. It was the one thing which
brought peace to his troubled mind. He was no
longer the idol of the distinguished and fash-
ionable. Almost everything was taken from
him; little remained except his painting mate-
rials and some plain clothes. One who knew him
and saw him often wrote: "He has become so
careless of his appearance that when at the easel
he wipes his brushes on the hinder portions of
his dress."

The shadows never lifted from over him.
Misfortune followed this genius to the end. He

died in deepest poverty, leaving nothing but "his clothes of wool and his working instruments." On the register of deaths in the Wester Kirk there is this simple entry: "Died, Tuesday, October 8, 1669, Rembrandt van Rijn, painter on the Roozegraft, opposite the Doolhof."

V

JOHN BUNYAN

JOHN BUNYAN was born in November, 1628, at Elstow, about a mile from Bedford, in England, on the road that stretches out toward London. His father was a tinker or mender of old brass. That his people were of the working class is evident from the fact that his grandmother at her death bequeathed to her people, "one brass pot" and "a standing bed in the loft."

It is not easy to find out how much time he spent at school. In one of his books he says he was sent to school "to learn me both to read and write the which I also attained according to the rate of other poor men's children." It is also well known that the schoolmaster at Bedford, where John probably attended, spent most of his time in alehouses and thus neglected his duties. Probably there were a great many more evil influences than good ones at work when Bunyan was a boy, and it is evident, from what he wrote later, that he formed many bad habits. This is his own confession, "Even as a child I had few equals in cursing, swearing, lying, and blaspheming the holy name of God." Even profane persons were shocked at his swearing.

JOHN BUNYAN

He was a young man during the days of the Civil War, and served in the army. While there he had an experience which made a profound impression upon him. He was one of a group selected to besiege a certain place. Another soldier who wanted to go pleaded with Bunyan to change places. Bunyan gave his consent, and this man, as he stood sentinel, was shot with a musket bullet and died. Bunyan returned to the little village of Elstow and married. Not much is known about his wife except that she was a sincere Christian woman who was frequently telling him about her father's virtues. Furthermore, when they married, we do know that they had very little, for he writes, "We were as poor as owlets without so much household stuff between us as a dish or a spoon." Evidently he continued to live in the humble circumstances in which he had been brought up as a boy.

Bunyan's wife had at least two books—one entitled *The Practice of Piety*, and the other, *The Plain Man's Pathway to Heaven*. These books had some influence upon him, for he writes that he tried hard to be "a right honest man," but only succeeded in becoming "a poor painted hypocrite." One day he was called to Bedford to work at his calling in one of the streets of the town. He came upon three or four poor women sitting at the door of a house in the street, talking about the things of God. He could not help overhearing what was being said, although he writes that he "heard but did not understand much for they talked about the work of God in their hearts." This conversation greatly impressed John Bunyan, and not long afterward he became a changed man. He forsook his profanity and evil ways of living, and joined the Baptist Meeting House at Bedford.

Bunyan began to preach about the year 1655, although evidently he continued to work at his trade. He was a man of great energy, enthusiasm, and passion. This is how he describes his own preaching, "I preached the terrors of the law for the guilt of my own transgressions lay heavy upon my conscience. I preached what I felt—*what I smartingly did feel*—even that under which my poor soul did groan and tremble to astonishment." After the Restoration in 1660 King Charles II came to the throne, and such men as Bunyan, who did not worship at the Church of England, were severely disciplined and forbidden to preach. The Conventicle Act passed in the reign of Queen Elizabeth was revived. It made the frequenting of such assemblies as Bunyan's congregation unlawful. On November 12, 1666, John Bunyan was to preach at Samwell, thirteen miles south of Bedford. He was warned, but persisted in going. When he approached the farmhouse where he was to preach, he was warned again, but it made no difference to him. He read from his Bible, and then preached. A constable and a magistrate who had a warrant for his arrest came in. He was arrested, and charged before the sessions with being an upholder of unlawful assemblies and conventicles and for not conforming to the national worship of the Church of England. He was sent to prison, where he remained for twelve years.

The prisons at that time were dark, evil-smelling, and miserable places, and yet they were crowded with men of piety and education. At one time there were as many as sixty non-conformists shut up in Bedford Jail for attending a religious meeting. Nevertheless, Bunyan seems to have been allowed a measure of freedom, for the record shows he was occasionally permitted to visit his own home and to preach secretly. Still a man of his great energy fretted considerably when compelled to refrain from the work which he loved and in which he was evidently very effective. In the jail he was permitted to carry on his trade as a tinker. He made laces which were sold for him in Bedford town, and by this means he managed to support his wife and children.

Bunyan had opportunities of gaining his release if he would solemnly promise to attend the national church and refrain from preaching.

This he refused to do. While being tried before Sir John Keeling, who later became Lord Chief Justice of England, the judge and Bunyan became involved in a bitter argument. Finally the judge said: "Hear your judgment. You must be had back again to prison, and there lie for three months following, and at three months' end if you do not submit to go to church and to hear divine service, and cease your preaching, you must be banished from the realm, and if after such a day as shall be appointed, you shall be found in this realm, or be found to come over again without special license from the King, you must stretch by the neck for it. I tell you plainly."

During the long weary days of his irksome imprisonment, John Bunyan's mind turned to scriptural themes, and he wrote several books now known the world over. The best known of these are, *The Pilgrim's Progress,* which was published in 1677, and *The Holy War.* After twelve years in prison Bunyan was pardoned in 1672, but was rearrested in May, 1675, and taken back to prison. It would seem to have been during the second imprisonment that *Pilgrim's Progress* was written in part, if not altogether. The book was bought and read by thousands. People of all shades of opinion read it. With the exception of the Bible, no book which ever

left the printing-press has been more widely circulated. It has been translated into one hundred
and eighteen languages. In all parts of the globe
it has been circulated and read by people of
every creed and nationality. Undoubtedly the
secret of the great success and universal appeal
of the book is that it is so true to life. Who has
not met such characters as "Mr. Worldly-Wise-
Man," "Mr. Facing-Both-Ways," "Mr. Plia-
ble," "Mr. Valiant-for-the-Truth"? Later John
Bunyan's *Holy War* was also widely read, but
Pilgrim's Progress remains the book by which
he will be remembered as long as the world
lasts.

He was finally released in 1680, and for the
remaining eight years of his life was a free man.
He was evidently in much demand as a
preacher, for one who heard him at that time
writes, "When Mr. Bunyan preached in London, if there was but one day's notice given,
there would be more people come together to
hear him preach than the meeting house could
hold. I have seen to hear him preach, about
twelve hundred at a morning lecture by seven
o'clock on a working day in the dark Winter-
time. I also computed about three thousand who
came to hear him one Lord's Day in London at
a Townsend meeting house so that half were
fain to go back again for want of room, and he

had to be pulled almost over the people to get upstairs to his pulpit."

John Bunyan died on Friday, August 31, 1688, and was buried in Bunhill Fields Cemetery in London. Thus closed the life of one who was born in poverty, and suffered imprisonment and persecution for the greater part of his life, yet left to the world a book which is probably the most quoted book of its kind ever written.

VI

WOLFGANG MOZART

WOLFGANG MOZART was born in the little town of Salzburg near Vienna on January 27, 1756. He was a delicate and extremely sensitive child who would ask his friends a dozen times a day if they loved him. If they answered, "No," as they sometimes did to tease him, he would burst into tears and for a while be inconsolable. His father, Leopold Mozart, was a musician engaged in the Bishop's Chapel at Salzburg. Though a gifted musician, Leopold Mozart never earned more than a very scanty living, being constantly dependent, as musicians were in those days, upon the favors of wealthy patrons.

Of the seven children born to Leopold Mozart and his wife, only two survived—Wolfgang and his sister Nannerl, who was five years older than her brother. The children were very happy and passionately fond of music. When the father was giving lessons to Nannerl, little Wolfgang, although only three years of age, would drop his toys and listen intently, taking in every word which was said to his sister. One afternoon when Nannerl was taking her lesson Wolfgang was especially attentive, but re-

WOLFGANG MOZART

mained as quiet as a mouse all through the lesson. When it was over he sat down at the piano and, to the amazement of his father and his sister, his baby fingers searched out the keys of his sister's exercises and played them correctly. The father, greatly excited, caught the little lad up in his arms and said, "Who would have thought that my little baby would have understood what I was teaching Nannerl?" The development of this child musician is one of the strangest and most fascinating stories in the whole history of music. In his fourth year he was taking lessons regularly from his father, and playing with a firmness and precision which astonished all who heard him. At that early age he would learn to play each Minuet correctly in half an hour.

Before he was five he had actually begun the composition of little musical pieces which his father wrote down in a music-book, now preserved in the Mozart collection at Salzburg. At the close of each musical composition the father would write some comment. These comments can still be seen. For instance, one reads such as the following: "This Minuet was learned by Wolfgang in his fourth year." Again, "This Minuet was learned by Wolfgang in half an hour the day before he reached his fifth birthday." And then this most astonishing of all occurs after a delightful little Minuet, "This was composed by Wolfgang on May 11th and July 16th, 1762." Thus this amazing boy was actually composing music when only six years of age. It is recorded that even at this time he could tell when one note of a violin was one-eighth of a tone lower than another.

Wolfgang made his first appearance in public on September 3, 1761, and created a sensation. On the 12th of January following, his father took him to Munich, where they remained three weeks. Here again the remarkable precocity of the child simply astounded those who heard him, some of whom were distinguished musicians. Many were ready to agree with his father, who said, "What it takes others months and years of very hard practice to learn comes to Wolfgang as a gift from God." Others, when they saw the little boy seated at the piano without the faintest sign of embarrassment, playing difficult pieces correctly, exclaimed, "This is nothing short of a miracle."

In September, 1762, Leopold Mozart set out for Vienna, taking Wolfgang with him, and Nannerl, who was also a gifted musician. The father's object in taking the children to Vienna was to have them play at the Imperial Palace. On the way there the Mozarts rested at the Monastery in Ybbs, a gray old building on the banks of the River Danube. In the chapel of this monastery there was a fine old organ, and little Wolfgang, who was just six at the time, viewed it with astonished eyes. Then he crept up into the loft, sat on the organ stool, and began to play. Three friars who were passing through the monastery heard the strains of music, and were so charmed that they drew near, expecting to see some dignified musician. When they saw the six-year-old child playing with the assurance and ease of a great musician, they could hardly believe their eyes or ears. When the little fellow saw he was discovered, he very quietly closed the organ and tiptoed away.

The Imperial family at Vienna were extraordinarily fond of music. Many of them were themselves talented musicians. It is not surprising that the Mozart children created from the very beginning a most favorable impression. The Emperor Francis I was especially interested in the little musician. He made Wolfgang play with only one finger, in which the child was perfectly successful. Then the keys of the piano were covered with a piece of cloth, and once again the six-year-old boy played faultlessly.

The little fellow would play for hours at a time, sitting with his delicate face and large soft eyes thinking of nothing but his music. In spite of the extravagant praise and favors heaped upon him, Wolfgang remained an unspoiled child, kind, sympathetic, and affectionate, one whose feelings were easily hurt by any kind of rebuke, but just as quickly healed by a few words of understanding and appreciation.

From Vienna the children were taken to Paris, and on New Year's Day, 1764, were presented at the Royal Court. At the table Wolfgang sat next to the Queen, who enjoyed the conversation of the little boy, but could scarcely believe that so young a child could be proficient in music. Wolfgang was granted permission to play the great organ in the King's Chapel and those who heard him play said he was equally great as organist and pianist. At this time the boy could accompany distinguished singers, rendering difficult selections, even though he had never seen the music previously.

From Paris the Mozarts went on to London, where their success was, if possible, greater than that of the French capital. They arrived in London on April 23, 1764, and four days later were invited to Buckingham Palace to play before the King and Queen. George III and his Queen were both very fond of music, and recognized the genius of Wolfgang Mozart at once. The king placed before young Wolfgang difficult pieces by Bach and Handel with the request that he would play them at sight. The perfect manner in which the eight-year-old boy rendered these selections so astonished the king that he insisted upon Wolfgang playing upon the organ, where he triumphed again. Dr. Burney, a great musician of that day, declared that there were few teachers of music even in middle life who could play with the ease and finish of the boy.

The family left London in July, 1765, when the first of many heavy misfortunes fell upon them. Both Wolfgang and his sister fell dangerously ill with a violent fever and it was many weeks before they could resume their travels. Finally, however, they returned to their home in Salzburg in November, 1765, after a tour which must ever rank as one of the greatest musical events in all history. They had been traveling for more than three years.

In spite of the success of the tour the Mozarts remained poor. They had received more praise than money, for the new archbishop was not a patron of music, and instead of looking with favor upon the Mozarts he placed every possible obstacle in their way. Added to this was the bitter jealousy of many older musicians who refused to believe the reports of the boy's genius. After spending some time in serious study at his home, Leopold Mozart thought it best to send the boy to Italy. There some of the greatest musicians in the world congregated, and it was said that no finer music could be heard anywhere than in its large cathedrals. He also wished Wolfgang to visit the great art galleries and study the paintings there. Everything about

Rome charmed and delighted Wolfgang—the brightly clad peasants walking along the streets or singing merrily at their work in the vineyards and sunny fields; the processions of richly robed priests passing along the narrow lanes of that historic city; and most of all the grand music from the wonderful organs in the cathedrals. One day during Holy Week Wolfgang went with his father and sister to the Sistine Chapel and heard a famous "Miserere" by Allegri. The music was permitted to reach only the musicians engaged in the chapel. It was never allowed to be taken outside. Many had asked permission to copy it, but had always met with stern refusal. A few had tried to write it from memory, but had failed. Young Wolfgang Mozart was thrilled with the music and after the service went to his home, wrote it out from memory, then concealed it in his cap and went and heard the music a second time so that he could correct any errors. A few days later he rendered the music before the master of the chapel choir whose name was Salaceti. This man was amazed and demanded to know who had secretly given the boy a copy of the music. When Wolfgang Mozart showed him what he had written, it was found the composition of the boy was identical with that used by members of the choir.

From Rome Mozart went to Naples, and there he gave a concert before a large audience.

While rendering one of his selections he noticed the people were uneasy and were whispering to one another. His father, who was present, learned the cause of the disturbance and explained it to his son. It appears that some people in the audience were so thrilled with his playing that they were saying that there was a charm in the diamond ring which he wore on his left finger. Wolfgang, very much amused, took the ring off, and played better than ever!

On August 4, 1772, Mozart married the daughter of a musician and settled in Vienna. Mozart and his wife were very fond of each other, but neither of them was practical enough to manage the affairs of a household. This, combined with the delicate health of his wife, meant that they knew a great deal of hardship and poverty. In fact it is one of the strange things that this remarkable man, undoubtedly one of the greatest musical geniuses in the history of the world, had one long bitter struggle with poverty. On one occasion when he was leaving to visit his father for the first time after his wedding, he was arrested for a debt of fifteen dollars just as he was about to step into the carriage. More than once he and his wife were on the verge of destitution, and only the intervention of friends prevented actual starvation. His expenses increased and his earnings became less. At one time he had only one pupil. He became involved in financial difficulties from which he could not extricate himself.

When Leopold II was crowned at Frankfort in October, 1790, Mozart was commanded to be present at court and take part in the musical program. In order to obtain the necessary funds, he was obliged to pawn what little silverware he had. Sometimes he received no pay for his work; occasionally he was cheated out of money that he did earn and so-called friends took advantage of his generous and sympathetic disposition.

One of the greatest musicians at that time was the composer Haydn. On one occasion Haydn took Leopold Mozart aside and said concerning his son, Wolfgang, "I tell you, by God, and as an honest man that I acknowledge your son to be the greatest composer of whom I have ever heard. He has taste and possesses the most thorough knowledge of composition." Coming from such a source this praise was deeply significant. Altogether Mozart wrote eight hundred works which included eighteen operas, forty-nine symphonies, fifteen overtures, seventy sacred compositions, and a vast number of uncompleted works left at death.

In spite of poverty and frequent ill health Mozart continued to compose with a feverish anxiety, hoping to extricate himself from his troubles, and to bring to his distressed wife and

family some of the comforts which other fami-
lies enjoyed. He was extravagant and probably
too fond of fine clothes and gay festivities, yet
he was a deeply religious man. He once said:

"As death, strictly speaking, is the true end
and aim of our lives, I have accustomed myself
during the last two years to so close a contem-
plation of this, our best and truest friend, that
he possesses no more terrors for me—nothing
but peace and consolation. And I thank God for
enabling me to discern in death the key to our
true blessedness. I never lie down in bed without remembering that, perhaps, young as I am,
I may never see another day, and yet no one
who knows me can say that I am melancholy or
fanciful. For this blessing I thank God daily,
and desire nothing more than to share it with
my fellow men."

One night in the middle of July, 1791, a
stranger visited Mozart—a tall, haggard-look-
ing man clothed in gray. He asked the musician
to compose a requiem which he said he wished
for his master. It turned out later that the man
was a servant of Count Franz von Walsegg and
the requiem was intended for his master's wife,
who had died earlier in the year. Mozart
worked with pathetic eagerness over the composition of this requiem, telling his wife that he
felt he was writing it for himself. It transpired
that in some sense this was true, for he was still

engaged in his composition late in the evening of December 4th when he lost consciousness. He died early in the morning of December 5, 1791.

On the following day his body was taken to the graveyard of St. Mark in Vienna. The weather became so bad that the mourners returned to their homes and no friend except the attendants of the cemetery stood by the grave of the man who by his wonderful art had prepared joy and pleasure for his fellow creatures. Afterwards his widow, who had been ill on the day of the funeral, visited the cemetery, but found there a new gravedigger who was unable to point out her husband's grave. All search proved fruitless, and one whom many considered to be the greatest musician of all time was buried in an unknown grave. He had filled the world with music, but had died in want and bitter sorrow.

VII

ROBERT BURNS

ROBERT BURNS, the Scottish poet, was born at
Alloway near Ayr in Scotland on January 25,
1759. The home in which he first saw the light
was a humble clay-built cottage, the work of his
father, who was a farmer in poor circumstances.
The poet's father met with a series of misfortunes from which he never was able to extricate
himself. His cattle suffered from accident and
disease, so that the family lived very sparingly.
For several years butcher's meat was a stranger
in the house, while every member of the family
worked to the utmost of his strength, if not be-
yond it, to help the family fortune.

At the age of thirteen Robert Burns threshed
the corn with his own hands. At fifteen he was
the principal laborer on the farm. No servant
was kept, and every one of the seven children,
of whom Robert was the eldest, soon became accustomed to hard work. As a boy Robert was
quite robust, but soon his physical strength was
overtaxed and his constitution received a shock
from which he never fully recovered. His shoulders stooped, he became liable to headaches and
subject to fits of melancholy. These trying bitter

ROBERT BURNS

days he never forgot, and later when he became a poet he put into verse what he had learned at the plow.

His days at school were few and irregular. However, there was some compensation in the fact that his father was an unusually thoughtful, industrious, and honorable man with a great love for his children and a deep concern for their welfare. One result of this was that Robert early became a great lover of books. He admits that, even when tired from hard work in the fields as a boy, he would eat his meals with a spoon in one hand and a book in the other. He carried some small volumes in his pocket to study in the few moments he could snatch while resting from his labors. He was especially fond of poetry, and would be reading a book of poems while sitting on the cart which he drove, or whistling at the plow. At night he lingered over the ballads in his cold room, and soon had committed to memory a great many of the hunting songs and ballads of his native land.

From earliest boyhood he was a great lover of nature. A walk in the woods exalted him, the song of a bird thrilled him. To walk through a plantation on a cloudy, wintry day, to hear the stormy wind howling among the trees and over the plain, awakened something in his soul that set him to the composition of verses even when he was as young as thirteen or fourteen.

Throughout his life this love of nature steadily increased until it became a passion with him. He compared himself to an Æolian harp strung to every wind of heaven. His sympathetic nature found charm and beauty in every living thing. The sight of a daisy, the singing of a bird, the disturbing of a mouse's nest, all suggested to him subjects for poems. He loitered by the streams of Afton Water, and in the murmuring of the brooks he heard a music deep down in his own heart. It is no wonder that one who was naturally so sympathetic should make many friends.

Burns was above everything else a lover of his fellow men, and yet many of the friendships which he formed were decidedly unfortunate. For instance, at this time he found a friend in a young sailor who was older than himself, and who had visited many lands but had formed evil habits. The friendship of this youth, who in some respects was likable enough, flattered Burns, but he spoke with levity of many things which Burns had been told to regard as sacred, and many years afterward, in writing of this part of his life, Burns said, regretfully, "His friendship did me a great mischief." It would seem as if at this period of his life Burns formed many friendships, some of which were good and helpful, but others were quite the reverse.

About this time Robert Burns and his brother Gilbert, who was two years younger than himself, leased a farm at Mossgiel. They both worked hard and lived on an allowance of thirty-five dollars a year each. Yet the venture proved to be very much of a failure. Just about this time his father died, an event which profoundly impressed and saddened Burns, who was not unmindful of the sterling, honest qualities of his noble parent.

Hoping to improve his fortune, Burns decided to emigrate to the West Indies, but he was penniless and needed money to carry out his plans. He had written many poems by this time, some of which appeared in a local newspaper and others had been sent to friends. A few he had in his own keeping. In his anxiety to gather sufficient money to go abroad, he accepted the suggestion of a friend that he should publish a book of poems. These poems were published on July 31, 1786, and the entire issue of six hundred copies was taken up so quickly that printers and binders could scarcely get them out fast enough.

The book created a sensation, and soon the whole countryside rang with the praises of the plowman whose poems—gay or pathetic, stern or tender in tone—touched the heartstrings of his people as no other poet had ever done. One living near at that time thus describes the reception given to this first edition of Burns' poems:

"Old and young, high and low, grave and gay, learned and ignorant—all were alike delighted, agitated, transported. I was at that time resident in Galloway, contiguous to Ayrshire, and I can well remember how that even plowboys and maidservants would have gladly bestowed the wages which they earned the most hardly, and which they wanted for necessary clothing, if they might but procure the works of Burns. A friend in my neighborhood put a copy into my hands on a Saturday evening. I opened the volume while I was undressing to go to bed, and closed it not till a late hour on the rising Sunday morn, after I had read over every syllable it contained."

Many poems issued in that volume had since become known and loved the world over. Among them were "The Cotter's Saturday Night"; "To a Mouse"; "Man Was Made to Mourn"; "Hallowe'en"; and many others.

Burns abandoned any thought of emigrating to the West Indies, and instead went to Edinburgh on November 28, 1786. His fame had preceded him, and his experience in Edinburgh society is one of the important periods of the poet's life. Everywhere he went he was received by persons of the highest rank, and made a great deal of. His natural genius, his strong good sense, his fine conversational powers, combined with a handsome appearance caused him to be the most-talked-of man of his country. The attention he received at this time would have turned the head of many a lesser man, but he retained through it all a simplicity of manner and a sense of dignity which stood him in good stead. At this time Sir Walter Scott was a boy in his early teens, and one day he was in a home where Burns was being lionized. Young Scott never forgot the simple and manly bearing of the plowman poet. He constantly referred to it in later years.

Burns wrote a second volume of poetry soon afterwards. More than three thousand copies were rapidly sold, which at that time was considered a great achievement. Among the list of subscribers were a number of eminent people, so that Burns had become accepted as one of the great poets of his generation. Many of the poems were of exquisite beauty. Such, for instance, as "To Mary in Heaven," "Ye Banks and Braes o' Bonnie Doon," "Auld Lang Syne," and "Duncan Gray," are sung not only wherever the English language is spoken, but in every land where maidens are wooed, where mothers lull their infants to sleep, where men toil in the open field or in the factory or workshop. In fact, wherever human beings work and toil and pray these songs are known and loved.

His hatred of hypocrisy caused Burns to say many bitter things, even about religious people.

At times he was abusive of those who differed from him. More than once he went too far and wrote what afterwards he wished unsaid. Nevertheless, Robert Burns had a firm belief in a supreme being. The tender memories of his home he set forth in his memorable poem, "The Cotter's Saturday Night," and what he felt about godlessness he expressed in the lines:

An atheist's laugh's a poor exchange
For Deity offended.

Burns' success as a poet did not improve his financial condition. Coupled with this was the fact that his weakened physical condition caused him such despondency that he foolishly resorted to stimulants and became somewhat intemperate in his habits. He became sour in temper and frequently plunged into dissipation. As a result he began to feel prematurely old. His hands shook, his pulse and appetite failed, and his spirits sank until in April, 1796, he wrote, "I close my eyes in misery, and open them without hope."

Early in July of that year he was seen to be dying. While lying on his bed sick and worried he received a letter threatening him with jail if he did not pay a certain debt he had incurred. This was a crushing blow to him, and one from which he did not recover. Rheumatism had attacked him in his early years. Long hours at the plow had damaged his heart, and a series of misfortunes had embittered him. On his death-bed he wrote a letter to his wife's father. Then he laid aside his pen forever. During the night and the two succeeding days the fever rose higher and higher, consuming what little strength he had and causing his mind to wander. When he did lapse into unconsciousness it is said he still muttered something about the threatening letter he had received and the disgrace of dying in debt.

He died on July 21, 1796, just a few months more than thirty-seven years of age, undoubtedly one of the greatest Scotsmen of all times. The clay-built cottage where he was born at Alloway, and which crosses the lovely River Doon about which he wrote, has become a place of pilgrimage to people who come from the ends of the earth to see where Robert Burns first saw the light. In the holiday season literally thousands of people visit that cottage every week, and his popularity grows rather than diminishes with the passing of the years. He was a poor man, in fact he died in debt, but he left the whole world richer.

VIII

OLIVER GOLDSMITH

IT IS not often that a boy who appears dull, and even stupid when at school, later in life becomes a great man. Such, however, happened in the case of Oliver Goldsmith. He was born in Ireland in 1728, the son of a poor clergyman who worked part of his time on his farm. When about six years of age Oliver nearly died of smallpox, and it set its mark upon him severely. His stature was small, and his limbs ill put together. In those days there was very little sympathy for a person who had physical defects, and whenever Oliver appeared among his playmates their ridicule was excited. He became the common butt of boys as well as teachers; he was pointed out in the playground as a boy who was a fright to look at, and when he entered the class-room he was punished as a dunce.

In his seventh year Oliver was sent to a village school kept by an old man who was a pensioner of the navy. This man seems to have been unable to teach anything except reading, writing, and arithmetic, but he had an inexhaustible fund of stories about ghosts and fairies, and as far as Oliver at least was concerned the teacher was quite satisfactory.

On the 11th of June, 1744, when Oliver was in his sixteenth year he was sent to Trinity College, Dublin, as a sizar. A sizar paid nothing for food and tuition, very little for lodging, but had to perform some manual services around the college. In Trinity College, which is still standing, there is a pane of glass with Oliver Goldsmith's name scribbled upon it. This is just the kind of thing Oliver was fond of doing. He never took advantage of any situation which opened to him, and was much more interested in playing than in studying. He neglected his studies to such an extent that he stood low in his examinations, and then was put at the bottom of the class for playing buffoon in the lecture-room, and also because he played a prank upon a local constable.

While Oliver was wasting his time at Dublin, his father died, leaving a widow and seven children. In February, 1749, Oliver obtained a degree and left the university. He went to live with his widowed mother. He was now in his twenty-first year. It was necessary that he should do something, but he had so wasted his time and frittered away his opportunities that he appeared incapable of doing anything but dress himself up in gay colors, sing Irish airs, and play the flute. In addition to this might be

OLIVER GOLDSMITH

added the gift of telling weird and impossible ghost stories. His mother was anxious that he should become a clergyman, and he applied for ordination, but he appeared before the bishop in scarlet clothes and he was very quickly turned out of the episcopal palace.

Later he decided to emigrate to America. By this time he had exhausted the patience of his relatives, and it was with a considerable amount of satisfaction that they saw him set out for Cork on a good horse, with one hundred and fifty dollars in his pocket. In six weeks he returned on a miserable old horse without a penny, and informed his mother that the ship on which he had taken his passage had sailed away while he was at a party. What his mother said is not recorded, but it is not likely it made much impression upon him, affectionate son though undoubtedly he was.

Later an uncle advanced him two hundred and fifty dollars and Oliver went to Dublin in order to study law. There he was enticed into a gambling-house and lost every cent. He decided to study medicine. Some friends got together and sent him to Edinburgh. He remained there for eighteen months, and picked up some superficial information about chemistry and natural history. Later he went to Leyden in Europe, still pretending to study for his doctor's degree. He left that university in his third year with a mere smattering of medical knowledge. All he had was the clothes he was wearing and a flute. In this way he traveled through Italy, France, Germany, and Switzerland. Afterward he wrote the wildest account of his travels, and it is hard to know how much was true and what was fiction. It is quite evident that he was a very jovial musician, but his hardest experiences were when he passed through a country where most people, as he confesses, could play the flute better than himself. He arrived at Dover in England in February, 1756, with only a few cents in his pocket. He was now twenty-eight years of age, and although he obtained some medical degree at Padua, it is evident that he had very little medical knowledge.

The uncle who had befriended him was dead. Most of his friends were weary of his irregular habits, and so when he arrived in London he was in desperate circumstances. He took a room in a tiny square in the heart of the city in Green Arbour Court. Here this restless, good-natured, but unlucky adventurer began to work like a galley slave in order to keep body and soul together. He wrote stories, articles, and reviews for magazines and newspapers. He compiled a number of children's books, some of which are still in existence, and he gradually rose in the estimation of booksellers for whom he drudged. His writing was not profound or even accurate, but he had a delightful way of stating in a clear and interesting manner his position. He wrote a history of England which was so charming as compared with the dull books previously written on that subject that children found it more interesting than any book of fiction. This was true of all his writing. Everything he touched he adorned.

He had a natural grace and ease in writing which soon caused him to rank as one of the greatest journalists of his day. It is amazing when one remembers the squalid circumstances in which Oliver Goldsmith lived at that time that his winged imagination should have completely triumphed over his surroundings. He wrote stories and essays that were amusing, descriptions that were picturesque, humor that was rich and joyous yet sometimes tinged with pathos, and all from a miserable little garret where he was so poor that, when a visitor came to see him, Oliver sat on the window-sill while his guest occupied the only chair in the room. There was practically no furniture. More often than not the windows were broken and patched with paper, yet in that room Goldsmith played his flute to ragged urchins, and sometimes sat down to write poetry and prose which will never be forgotten.

More than once he was quite unable to pay his milk bill. He was always willing to lend a helping hand to his poor neighbors, who frequently took advantage of his disposition. His visits to the pawnbrokers were frequent. His own clothes were often so wretched that he worked in his garret during the day and only ventured forth under cover of darkness, for he was naturally sensitive, and the sneers of well-dressed people hurt his feelings very much. He would find his way to some coffee house, and there would soon forget his poverty in friendly conversation and laughter. He must often have walked London streets and watched well-dressed ladies and gentlemen riding past in their coaches. All of this furnished him with material for his poems and stories.

In Christmas week, 1764, Goldsmith published a poem entitled "The Traveller." This did much to establish his growing reputation as a writer, but evidently did little to help him extricate himself from financial difficulties. A short time before this he had made the acquaintance of the great literary figure, Samuel Johnson. Johnson and Goldsmith were as different as two men could be. Johnson was serious and formal—every sentence he uttered packed with shrewdness and a knowledge of human nature. Goldsmith, on the other hand, always saw the funny side of things, and it was difficult to get him to be serious for very long. Yet the two were close friends.

One morning Dr. Johnson received a hurried message from Oliver Goldsmith saying that the latter was in great distress and needed assistance. Johnson, as usual, was quickly moved, and sent his friend five dollars and a message that he would be along to see him as soon as he could get dressed. He hurried over to Goldsmith's lodgings, and found the landlady had sent for the sheriff and arrested the poet for debt. Goldsmith told Johnson that he had a novel just completed. Johnson quickly glanced over the manuscript, saw it had great merit, and went out to a bookseller and sold it for three hundred dollars, and returned to his friend with the money. This manuscript was of *The Vicar of Wakefield*, one of the greatest novels in the English language. It has been read with approval by the people of a score of nationalities, and undoubtedly will remain a classic. The great German scholar Goethe considered it to be one of the greatest novels ever written. It has a very simple plot. It describes the family life of a poor Yorkshire clergyman, his wife and six children, and while it has no exciting scenes, it was written in such a way as to captivate readers.

In 1770 Goldsmith published a poem, "The Deserted Village." This described a village first in its happy days, and later on when prosperity had departed and it was in ruins. No doubt, in this wonderful poem Goldsmith had woven into the story an account of his own beloved father and his brother Henry, recently deceased, and had also made good use of his own bitter experiences walking the streets of a great city, friendless, poor, and ignored. Some passages in it are among the finest in the language, and have been quoted thousands of times. Goldsmith followed this literary success by writing a number of plays, including "She Stoops to Conquer" and "The Good-natured Man." He was not always successful with these plays, but by this time his work was in such demand that publishers were willing to pay in advance for what he promised to do.

Unfortunately, Oliver Goldsmith remained as improvident as ever—extravagant in his own habits, and easily imposed upon by others. Added to this was the fact that all his life he had been something of a gambler, and an unskilful one at that. He found himself deeper than ever in debt. He obtained advances from booksellers by promising to execute works for them which he had never begun. At one time he actually owed over ten thousand dollars, a vast sum in those days. Then the strain began to wear upon him. His naturally high spirits forsook him as the creditors came to his door and insisted upon payment.

In his forty-sixth year he was attacked by a nervous fever of which he thought he could cure himself. He refused to call in a competent physician, but his weakness and restlessness continued. He could get no sleep, and partook of little food. He tried to prescribe for himself, and became worse. At last a physician came to see him and said: "You are getting worse. Is your mind at ease?" "No, it is not," said Goldsmith. These were his last words. He died on the 4th of April, 1774, in his forty-sixth year. He was laid in the Temple Churchyard, but the place was not marked by any inscription and has long since been forgotten.

All his friends were deeply moved at his passing. They knew his weaknesses, but, spendthrift though he was, he was one of the most lovable characters of his day—generous, unselfish, and affectionate. The day he was buried the little house where he had lived and the steps outside were crowded to overflowing with the poor and outcast people whom he had befriended. There is a monument to his memory in Westminster Abbey, the epitaph of which was written by Samuel Johnson. The eulogy describes Goldsmith as "A poet, naturalist and historian who left scarcely any style of writing untouched, and touched nothing that he did not adorn."

IX

SAMUEL JOHNSON

ONE day in May, 1737, a young man named Samuel Johnson left his home in Lichfield, England, and went to London, hoping to earn his living there as a journalist. He must have looked a strange figure as he shuffled along the streets of that crowded city. His face was heavily marked with scrofula, and as he walked along the streets his big lanky frame was shaken with convulsive jerks, so that the sympathy or ridicule of passers-by must have been aroused.

He was born at Lichfield on September 18, 1709, the son of a poor bookseller and bookbinder. When he was two and a half years old his mother, with ten dollars sewed in her skirt so that nobody could steal it, went to London so that the boy might touch the garments of Queen Anne and be healed of the scrofula which so disfigured him. People were superstitious in those days, but touching the queen evidently did not do Samuel any good, for afterwards he became blind in one eye, and with the other could not see more than a few words. These things prevented him from entering into and enjoying sports with other boys. He attended a school kept by a widow, and was so attentive to his studies that when he left she gave him a present of gingerbread, and told him he was the best scholar she had ever had.

He was naturally an inquisitive boy, and had a wonderful memory. One day while he was still very young his mother gave him the Prayer Book, and told him to learn a certain prayer. She had scarcely got upstairs when he called after her, telling her he could repeat it perfectly after reading it through twice. This memory stood him in good stead, for in later years one who knew him well once said, "Samuel Johnson never forgets anything that he has heard."

When he was nineteen years of age he entered Pembroke College, Oxford, where he acted as servant. Sometimes his duties prevented him from attending the lectures, but some friends were kind enough to let him see their notes. He must have been a sorry figure in those days, for his shoes were worn out, his clothes were shabby to the point of being almost rags, and sometimes he was so embarrassed that he did not care to sit in lectures with the other students. At the end of three years he became so poor that he was obliged to leave college altogether. His father died soon afterward.

When he was twenty-six years old this lonely man, ungainly in appearance almost to the point of being ugly, fell in love with a widow forty-

SAMUEL JOHNSON

eight years of age. After obtaining his mother's consent he married her, and the union proved a happy one. His wife had a little money, and Samuel established a school and advertised for pupils, but only three came, and the school was closed. It was then that he decided to try London, and went there one day in May, 1737, leaving his wife behind in Lichfield for the time being.

London is a great city, and there have been a vast number of men who have walked its streets sad, lonely, and discouraged. Samuel Johnson was one of them. Sometimes he found himself without a home at night, and walked the streets until morning because he had no money for a lodging. He managed to live on nine cents a day. When he applied at the office of a publisher for a position, the man looked at him, and then told him frankly he thought he stood a better chance of earning a livelihood as a porter carrying trunks. He became discouraged, and applied for a country school where the salary was three hundred dollars a year, but he was unsuccessful even in that venture.

He submitted a manuscript to a publisher named Bernard Lintot, who paid him five dollars for it, and gave him an agreement to write a few more articles. This was the best encouragement Johnson had received since his arrival in London. He took the money and with a friend enjoyed a good breakfast, Johnson being in especially good spirits after misfortunes had made him heartsick. He published a poem entitled "London," which attracted the attention of some literary men. Soon afterward he was given a position on *The Gentleman's Magazine* and readers quickly recognized that he was a man of unusual ability. When he was forty he published an article entitled "The Vanity of Human Wishes," for which he received seventy-five dollars, and he began to feel that he had turned a corner and that fame was slowly coming to him. Afterwards he wrote *The Lives of the Poets*, which quickly became a classic.

About this time his wife died, and Johnson was so grief-stricken that he retired to the garret where he did his writing, and tried to banish his sorrow by concentrating on his work. He kept his wife's wedding ring in a little box until his death. In 1755 Samuel Johnson published his "Dictionary," a stupendous task over which he had worked for several years. When one considers his defective eyesight and other handicaps under which he labored, it is difficult to understand how one man could have compiled such a vast work and have done it accurately. The "Dictionary" brought him fame almost immediately. The Universities of Oxford and Dublin, when he no longer needed their assistance, bestowed degrees upon him. Even King George

III invited him to the royal palace. He was still, however, far from wealthy, for when his mother died he wrote a book, *Rasselas,* in the evenings of one week, for which he received three hundred dollars. This was the only way he managed to pay his mother's funeral expenses. For her he always had the tenderest regard, and there are few more touching letters in all literature than the following, which he wrote to her on one occasion:

DEAR HONOURED MOTHER—Neither your condition nor your character make it fit for me to say much. You have been the best mother, and I believe the best woman in the world. I thank you for your indulgence, and beg forgiveness of all that I have done ill, and all that I have omitted to do well. God grant you His Holy Spirit, and receive you to everlasting happiness, for Jesus Christ's sake. Amen. Lord Jesus receive your spirit. Amen.

I am, dear, dear mother,

Your dutiful son,
SAM JOHNSON.

When he was compiling his "Dictionary" Samuel Johnson was faced with many difficulties, one of which was financial. He tried hard to interest the Earl of Chesterfield in his project. This man, who could easily have helped Johnson, always managed to evade the author. Many of the saddest experiences in Johnson's life were the weary hours he spent waiting for an audience with the Earl of Chesterfield. At last, disappointed and discouraged, he turned away from the earl's door, and decided to write the "Dictionary" unassisted. When, some years later, the "Dictionary" was published and the whole world recognized what a marvelous work it was, the Earl of Chesterfield hastened to compliment Johnson on his work. There can be few more stinging rebukes in history than that which Johnson gave to the patronizing earl in the following letter:

Is not a Patron, my Lord, one who looks with unconcern on a man struggling for life in the water, and when he has reached ground, encumbers him with help? The notice which you have been pleased to take of my labours, had it been early, had been kind; but it has been delayed till I am indifferent, and cannot enjoy it; till I am solitary, and cannot impart it; till I am known and do not want it. I hope it is no very cynical asperity, not to confess obligations where no benefit has been received, or to be unwilling that the Publick should consider me as owing that to a Patron, which Providence has enabled me to do for myself. Having carried on my work thus far with so little obligation to any favourer of learning, I shall not be disappointed though I should conclude it, if less be possible, with less.

In 1762 Samuel Johnson was granted a modest pension. While this did not make him by any means a rich man, it removed the burden of poverty which he had borne for more than fifty years. It enabled him to do what he had wanted all his life to do, namely, render assistance to deserving people. He took care of a blind woman, the only claim she had upon him being that she had been a friend to his wife, and was in the house when she died. One day he found a poor woman late at night sick on the street, took her to his home, and kept her there until she was restored to health. He frequently gave all the coppers and silver he had in his pockets to street arabs and others who learned to watch for his passing. Sometimes when he found children asleep on doorsteps, as was common in those days, he would slip money into their hands so that when they awakened they might buy a breakfast. He was a great lover of London. That wonderful city has never had one who loved it more. He walked its streets at all hours of the day and night, and once said, "A day out of London is a day out of life."

Samuel Johnson died in London on December 13, 1784. He was kind to the last. To a lady who hastened to his bedside in order that she might ask his blessing, the great man said, "God bless you, my dear." These were his last words. He was buried with proper honor in Westminster Abbey, and monuments were erected to his memory at Lichfield, his birthplace, and in St. Paul's Cathedral.

X

THOMAS HOOD

THOMAS HOOD was born in London, England, on May 23, 1799. With the exception of three years spent in Scotland for the sake of his health, when he was in his teens, and some visits to Europe later on, he remained in London until his death. From his earliest childhood Thomas Hood was possessed of a mischievous spirit. In fact, in some respects he never seemed to grow up. When he became a man and had a home of his own, he was just as fond of playing harmless pranks as when he was a boy of eight or ten. He was fond of saying that the severest thrashing he ever got when at school was for reading a book, and then he used to add with a twinkle in his eyes, "This book was *Robinson Crusoe*." He read it when he was supposed to be doing his lessons.

He was taken from school early in life, and given work at the office of a merchant, but a breakdown in health made a change of occupation necessary. All his life Hood was in very delicate health. Yet the amazing thing is while sometimes he had scarcely sufficient physical energy to walk around, he utterly refused to be downhearted. There can have been very few men at any time in the world's history who gave more genuine pleasure to other people and made them laugh as often and as heartily as Thomas Hood, and yet his whole life was one constant battle with disease.

When he was fifteen years of age he was sent to stay with some relatives at Dundee in Scotland, where he remained for two years. Years afterwards his aunt, Mrs. Keay, with whom he stayed, and her son remembered what a mischief-loving boy Tom was. One Sunday his aunt was ill and unable to go to church. She asked Tom to describe the church-goers as they passed her window. His descriptions were so highly colored and extravagant that her eyes opened wider and wider in astonishment, and at last at some wild description she could no longer keep still, and in spite of her aches and pains got out of her seat and made her way across to the window, where she found that there was more fiction in Tom's description than truth. Her illness prevented her from giving him the spanking she thought he deserved.

In 1817, when he was eighteen years of age, he returned to London, where he became a regular contributor, chiefly of humorous articles, to magazines. The uncertain condition of his health made it impossible for him to do hard physical labor, but his wonderful poetic gift

THOMAS HOOD

and sense of humor enabled him to find his way into print, and when his mother died, his father having died previously, Tom found himself the main support of his four bereaved sisters. He was given a position as sub-editor of *The London Magazine*.

Soon his poems and articles in this magazine attracted such widespread attention that he became recognized as one of the leading literary men of Great Britain. He counted among his friends such distinguished men as Charles Lamb, Hartley Coleridge, D. Quincey, and Charles Dickens. Probably there has never been a writer who was more adept at making witty puns than Thomas Hood. He used to say, "One has to be a lively Hood in order to earn a livelihood." He wrote literally hundreds of puns somewhat like this, and this habit he continued throughout life. There was nothing bitter or sarcastic about him. He was kind, sympathetic, and generous. He found it exceedingly difficult to keep from making puns even on the most solemn occasions.

He was married on May 5, 1825, and established a home of his own. Fortunately, his daughter left an account of some of the family doings, which were quite typical of the humorist who was also a true genius. One day Mr. George Reynolds, Hood's father-in-law, was staying with him in his London home, which was in the midst of a delightful garden. Some boys were caught robbing the orchard and were brought trembling into the house. No kinder man than Thomas Hood ever lived, but he decided to have some fun with the young culprits. He persuaded Mr. Reynolds, who was a tall, imposing, heavily-built man, to pretend that he was a judge, and the boys were brought before the supposed judge, while Hood solemnly told of their theft. Then very solemnly the judge ordered them to be executed by hanging from a near-by cherry tree. The boys did not know it was a joke, and dropped on their knees, crying with fright. Amid their sobs they vowed they would "never do it no more." Hood's daughter never forgot their tremendous relief when they were told they could go, and how quickly they got out of the front door.

Fanny Hood, for that was his daughter's name, in later years remembered a hundred similar instances. She recalled that once her father had painted pink spots on the face of her favorite doll and told her that the poor thing was suffering from a severe attack of measles and she must not go near it. Though she was aching to comfort the sick doll, she could remember how she kept several feet away from it for several days until the spots had all vanished. She was not very old when she learned to suspect Dad was playing a prank when anything went wrong with the household affairs.

Hood published two books at this time which met with a very fine reception. These were *Odes and Addresses* and *Whims and Oddities*. Many of the charming little humorous poems and ballads in these books became favorites throughout the English-speaking world, and most have been recited at concerts and entertainments hundreds of times. Some of the best known of these ballads are "Sally Brown"; "Nelly Gray"; "Tim Turpin"; and "The Irish Schoolmaster." There was never anything forced about his humor. It just bubbled from him like something that could not be kept back. Later Thomas Hood edited a magazine, *Hood's Magazine and Comic Miscellany,* a very large part of which he wrote himself.

He had a marvelous faculty of rising above trouble. In spite of a sickly constitution and severe financial troubles, he managed to make a whole generation of people better for reading his writings. As he grew older the note of sadness began to appear in some of his poems, but he was never one to dwell upon his troubles. About this time he wrote a long poem, "The Dream of Eugene Aram." This was truly the work of genius and placed him at once in the forefront of English poets. It was translated into several languages and did much to make him famous.

Then something happened which caused him to write what was perhaps his greatest poem, and one which will never be forgotten. On October 25, 1843, a wretched woman was charged in a London police office with having pawned some articles belonging to her employer. It was shown that she had made trousers for sevenpence a pair, and that the utmost she could make by working her best in a week was seven shillings. The poor woman was trying to support herself and two infant children on this amount. Hood, whose heart was deeply stirred by the incident, and whose indignation against the employers was justly aroused, sent to the famous magazine, *Punch,* a poem entitled "The Song of the Shirt." It was published in the Christmas number for that year. It sold in the most emphatic fashion. It was copied into hundreds of newspapers and journals. As one writer of that time said, "It spread through the land like wildfire." Not only in England was the poem popular, but newspapers in France, Germany, Italy, and many other countries translated the poem, and it did more than any other literary work of that age to stir up indignation against the frightful conditions which obtained in the sweatshops of Europe. The editor of *Punch* himself acknowledged that "The Song of the Shirt" trebled the circulation of the journal.

Some time after this Thomas Hood wrote another famous poem, "The Bridge of Sighs," the tender and appealing story of a heart-broken woman. That Thomas Hood the humorist should write poems in which the melancholy note was so pronounced caused not a little surprise, and yet those who knew his tenderness and sympathy understood such poetry was as natural from him as was his humor.

Hood then wrote a volume of serious poems. Nothing saddened him more than to find that the public did not welcome this volume. They had looked upon him for many years as a fun-maker. His puns had made them laugh. His harmless jokes had brightened the day for thousands, and they wanted him to keep on doing that kind of thing. The refusal of the public to accept him as a writer of serious poetry was one of the most crushing blows that Hood ever received.

Hood was not as successful in financial matters as he was in literary affairs. Many of the ventures involved him in debt. Even at the time when he was so well and favorably known, he became utterly bankrupt. Like so many men of genius, he was not practical in managing the affairs of his household. He was generous to a fault, and did not realize how poor he was until disaster completely overtook him. His friends urged him to declare himself bankrupt, but, like the illustrious Sir Walter Scott, he determined to pay off his debts, and to use every ounce of strength he had in doing so. He sold all the effects that he could part with, and still have a home left, then began to meet his obligations. In this he was only partially successful. A severe breakdown culminating in his death made it impossible for him to fulfill his wishes.

In the spring of 1845 he realized that he could not live very long. He saw the oncoming of death, and met it with great cheerfulness. The friends who visited him were deeply touched by his unwillingness to utter any complaints, or even to allow them to discuss too sadly his condition. To one, however, he said: "This is a beautiful world, and since I have been lying here, I think of it more and more. I have had some very happy days while I lived in it. Certainly I could have wished to stay a little longer, but it is all for the best, and we shall all meet again in a better world."

On May 1st, knowing himself to be dying, he called his family around him—the patient, loving wife of twenty years, the daughter of fifteen, and the son of ten, and spoke a very tender farewell. Soon afterwards he lapsed into unconsciousness, and passed away peacefully on the morning of Saturday, May 3rd. On his death-bed he wrote some verses which beautifully express his faith in the hereafter, for he was a truly religious man. These verses may be taken as the "Swan-song" of a great sufferer, but one who never complained:

> *Farewell, Life! My senses swim;*
> *And the world is growing dim;*
> *Thronging shadows cloud the light,*
> *Like the advent of the night,—*
> *Colder, colder, colder still*
> *Upward steals a vapour chill—*
> *Strong the earthy odour grows—*
> *I smell the Mould above the Rose!*
>
> *Welcome, Life! the Spirit strives!*
> *Strength returns, and hope revives;*
> *Cloudy fears and shapes forlorn*
> *Fly like shadows at the morn,—*
> *O'er the earth there comes a bloom—*
> *Sunny light for sullen gloom,*
> *Warm perfume for vapour cold—*
> *I smell the Rose above the Mould!*

XI

HENRY DAVID THOREAU

ABOUT ninety years ago a great nature-lover built a home in the solitary woods at Walden, Massachusetts. This man, whose name was Henry David Thoreau, loved and understood birds, animals, and flowers as few men have ever done. Sometimes when walking with friends he would surprise them by plunging his hand in the water and bringing up a fine large fish which lay contentedly in his hand as if they were old acquaintances.

He would sit patiently for hours on a rock near the water until the bird or reptile or fish which had retreated from him should come back and resume its habits. One thing which greatly pleased him was the way in which the wild birds ceased to be afraid of him, so that when he was digging in his garden they would perch on his shoulder and even upon his spade. He used to say that he felt more honored by the friendship of these birds than if an emperor had conferred a distinction upon him.

Henry David Thoreau was born at Concord, Massachusetts, in 1817. He was sent to Harvard University and graduated in 1837. The only thing which distinguished him at college was the fact that he loved to do things in his own way and delighted to ramble in the woods, where he found scores of things that filled him with wonder. While still in his 'teens he had gathered a remarkable collection of specimens of natural history.

After leaving college he secured a position as a school-teacher in Concord. In those days the slightest inattention or mischief on the part of a pupil was followed by severe punishment. Sometimes, for a very slight thing, a boy would be so severely flogged that he ached for days. Thoreau was naturally kind and sympathetic, so refused to follow these customary ways of treating pupils. When members of the school board complained because he did not flog the boys, he resigned his position, and he and his brother established a school of their own where they were free to follow their own methods.

Everything about the Thoreau school was different from the town school. They made the recess half an hour long instead of a few minutes. They opened the windows and ventilated the rooms so that the boys came back after their playing to freshly-aired rooms. They never thrashed the pupils; if the lesson seemed dull, they would tell a story, at which both brothers were wonderfully apt. Not only did the boys

HENRY DAVID THOREAU

relish this change, but they made so much more progress with their studies than those at the town school that parents, who had been critical at first, now sent their children to the Thoreau school in such numbers that there was always a long waiting list.

It was in 1845 that Henry Thoreau built his cottage in Walden Wood near a lake, so that he might more closely study nature. He purchased the boards of an Irishman's shanty and with his own hands soon had his cabin built, snug and neat. "It seems to me," he said, "that a man should enjoy building his own home as a bird does building its nest."

Thoreau loved simple things. He was generous, always willing to share what he had with others, but he detested foolish and extravagant ways of living. He never wasted anything. Practically every piece of furniture in his cabin he made himself. While living in his forest home he was happier than any king in his palace and wrote a really great nature-study book. He said: "When I wrote that book I lived alone in the woods, a mile from any neighbor, in a house which I had built myself on the shores of Walden Pond and I earned my living with my hands only. My home was on the side of a hill in the midst of young forest pines and hickories, and only half a dozen rods from the pond. In front of my cabin grew the strawberry, black-berry, goldenrod, scrub-oaks, blueberry and ground-nut."

He made his own bread, first of Indian meal and salt, baked over a fire out-of-doors on a shingle or on the end of a piece of lumber sawed off in building his house. He would try half a dozen ways of baking bread, laughing heartily at himself when it was a failure, and chuckling merrily when it was palatable.

Henry Thoreau went into the woods to study nature, but it sometimes seemed to him as if the creatures of the forest had made up their minds to study him. They lost all fear of him, and he could scarcely move out of his cabin door without attracting their attention. Mice playfully ate out of his fingers; even the furtive mole paid him friendly visits. Sparrows came when he called them, and alighted on his shoulder, and the wild partridge with her brood visited him, as one neighbor to another.

Writing of the mice which watched him erect his house, he said, "When I was building, one of these mice had its nest underneath the house, and would come out regularly at lunch-time and pick up the crumbs at my feet. It probably had never seen a man before; it soon became quite familiar and would run over my shoes and up my clothes. . . . It ran round and round the paper which held my dinner while I kept the latter close, and dodged and played bo-peep with it. When, at last, I held a piece of cheese between my thumb and fingers it came and nibbled it, sitting in the palm of my hand, afterwards cleaning its face and paws like a fly, then walking away."

It seemed as if he had some magnetic attraction for these little animals, for sometimes when he wanted to free himself from their attentions he was helpless to do so. One day he took a squirrel into his cabin in order to study its habits. Then he wanted it to return to the trees, but it had no intention of doing so. More than once he took it to the tree where he had found it, but it absolutely refused to be left there. At length it hid its head in the folds of his vest, and that was a sign of affection he could not resist, so he took it home with him.

Many distinguished men visited Thoreau in his woodland home. Among them was William E. Channing. He wrote: "Thoreau named all the birds without a gun, a weapon he never used in mature years. He neither killed nor imprisoned any animal unless driven by actual need. He possessed such remarkable topographical instincts that he could conceal things in the bush and easily find them again. He never got lost in the woods. If he needed a box in his walk, he would strip a piece of birch bark from a tree, fold it when cut straightly, and put his tender lichen or other little creature therein."

Another famous man, Ralph Waldo Emerson, visited Thoreau, and was amazed at the naturalist's ingenuity. He wrote: "It was a pleasure and a privilege to walk with him in the woods. He knew the country like a fox or a bird, and passed through it freely by paths of his own. Generally he carried an old book in which he pressed plants that interested him. He would take from his pocket a diary and read the names of all plants that should bloom that day. He thought that if he were suddenly waked up from a long trance in the swamp he could tell, within two days, what time of the year it was, by looking at the plants around him. He was not only interested in flowers, birds, and animals; he loved them and felt that they were his friends and companions. He could pace distances more accurately than another man could by rod and chain. He could find his way in the woods by night better by his feet than by his eyes. He knew every track in the snow and on the ground, and what creature had taken the path in the snow before him."

For many years Thoreau wrote articles for magazines telling of the wonderful things he had learned as he studied nature. As a boy at

school, and later at college, he had found great
delight in writing essays. His style was easy to
read, and soon he was recognized as an author-
ity in nature study. Later he published the
result of his observations in book form, and altogether he wrote thirty volumes, every one
characterized by that painstaking labor and ac-
curacy which made him one of the leading
naturalists in the world.

He loved simplicity in life. A more simple
and natural man it would be hard to find. He
disliked show, and vanity in any form was foreign to his nature. Always he wore the plainest
kind of clothing. He had no interest whatever in
hoarding money or multiplying worldly goods.
His frugal needs were easily met; he was rich
only in kindness and tender sympathy. Great
cities, with some people living extravagantly,
while thousands suffered acute poverty, made
him both sad and indignant. His big heart was
full of sympathy, and any story of suffering
caused him distress.

He trusted men and women utterly, and they
responded to his friendliness, just as birds and
animals did. Speaking of the time he lived in
the woods, he said: "I was never molested by
any person. I had no lock or bolt but for the
desk which held my papers, not even a nail put
over my latch or windows. I never fastened the

door night or day, though I was often absent several days at a time and on one occasion, at least, for two weeks. My house was more respected than if it had been surrounded by a regiment of soldiers."

On November, 1860, he took a severe cold while counting the rings on trees and when there was snow on the ground. A bronchial affection set in and caused him great pain, which he bore uncomplainingly. His friend, W. E. Channing, wrote: "With an unfaltering trust in God's mercies and never deserted by his good genius, he bravely bore the pains of his terrible malady, working steadily to the last. He lingered on till the following spring, and died on the morning of May 3, 1861."

One who was present at the funeral wrote: "While we walked in procession up to the church, though the bell tolled the forty-four years he had lived, we could not really believe that he was dead whose ideas and sentiments were so vivid in our souls. The band of friends reverently lowered the body into the bosom of mother earth, on the pleasant hillside of his native village, amidst the haunts he loved so well:

There will yet his mother yield
A pillow in her greenest field,
Nor the pure flowers scorn to cover,
The clay of their departed lover.

Home Sweet Home
by John Howard Payne

'Mid pleasures and palaces though we may roam,
Be it ever so humble, there's no place like home.
A charm from the skies seems to hallow us there,
Which, seek through the world, is ne'er met with elsewhere!

An exile from home, splendor dazzles in vain;
Oh, give me my lowly thatched cottage again.
The birds singing gaily that came at my call,
Give me them with the peace of mind dearer than all.

How sweet 'tis to sit 'neath a fond father's smile,
And the cares of a mother to soothe and beguile.
Let others delight 'mid new pleasures to roam,
But give me, oh, give me, the pleasures of home.

To thee I'll return overburdened with care,
The heart's dearest solace will smile on me there;
No more from that cottage again will I roam—
Be it ever so humble, there's no place like home.

XII

JOHN HOWARD PAYNE

MORE than a century ago, a ten-year-old boy living in Boston was told by some friends that he had a double crown on his head and that he would cross seas and see strange lands. The little fellow, whose name was John Howard Payne, was thrilled at such a prospect. He little realized at that time how much of a traveler he was to be and what a very long exile he would have from his home.

John Howard Payne was born in Boston on June 9, 1792. His father was principal of a small teaching academy in that city. He was one of a large family, and from his earliest days had a close acquaintance, if not with actual poverty, with something very near to it. When he was fourteen years of age he was sent to Union College, where he earned a little toward his expenses by writing poems and essays for neighboring newspapers. In October, 1806, he wrote a poem entitled "Home" which expressed his intense affection for his people and a great longing to see more of them.

His father's failing health made it necessary for the lad to launch out into the world when he was less than sixteen. He was at that time the oldest living son in the family. At seventeen he went on the stage, but soon abandoned the life of an actor and tried to support himself by his writings.

In 1813 he went to London, and some time afterwards on to Paris. The greater part of the remainder of his life was spent between these two cities. He tried to make his living as a playwright, and altogether wrote more than sixty plays, some of which were quite successful. He lived a life filled with strange vicissitudes, sometimes being in fairly good circumstances, but more often than not suffering from such financial distress that it developed in him a sad and melancholy strain.

In 1820 he took over the management of the Sadler Wells Theatre in London. He was hopeful of doing well, but the venture failed dismally and Payne was committed to Fleet Street prison in London until he could satisfy the claims of his creditors. He was at that time just twenty-eight years of age and of a kindly and extremely sensitive disposition. He felt keenly the humiliation and disgrace of having to write to his home in America from behind prison walls. He was permitted to live in the district known as "Rules of the Fleet," and secured lodgings in an alley known as "Naked Boy Court." Fortunately, many of the letters written by Payne to his relatives in America have been preserved, and it is possible to gain an insight into the gentle soul of this song-writer during these distressing days.

On January 2, 1821, he wrote from prison: "There may be some advantage even in our mistakes. He that has struck upon a rock in one voyage, may fix upon his memory where he found that rock and avoid it when he sails again. The faults of one year, if remembered in the next, may not be such a great misfortune after all. Now at the beginning of this new year I think I see clearer than ever how I can do better in the future. On looking into my soul I find its eternal interests have been neglected, and are in a state of chaos. . . . I have neglected to read the Bible, and am almost ignorant of it. I am determined to correct this. It will be at least one point gained if at the end of this year I can truthfully say that I am well versed in the Bible.

"I am now nearly thirty years of age, and am worse off than I have ever been before. I am in prison, and deeper than ever in debt, yet I have labored and suffered much. I need more prudence, more economy and punctuality in my way of living."

A few weeks later he wrote: "To-day I sent my shirt to the pawnbrokers, and got enough money to buy the day's provisions. Time is a great humbler. Twelve years ago I thought myself much more of a man than I do now. Sometimes I feel as if I were settling down into a quiet, inoffensive life—or perhaps I am settling down into poverty."

After his release from prison he worked harder than ever to extricate himself from the difficulties into which he had fallen. He was somewhat successful, for two years later, in writing to Thatcher Payne, his brother, in New York, he said: "After I got back to France matters went on so hopelessly as to leave me in a state next to starvation, and I should have perished but for some accidents of a fortunate character. Now my fortunes seem to have taken a better turn. I am not at present in fear of being gnawed at by hungry creditors. This gives me at least some feeling of independence. I hope I have been improved by the lessons of suffering, and that I shall add to my little stock by industry until I have a better place in the world."

All the letters written by John Howard Payne at this time express with unusual feeling and pathos his affection for home and the dear ones he had left behind. He wandered around the streets of Paris as he had done previously in London, weary and homesick, penniless, and friendless, fighting what seemed at times to be a losing battle against misfortune and poverty. This is reflected in nearly every letter he wrote. In this one, for instance:

"My yearnings toward home become stronger as the term of my exile lengthens. I long to see all your faces and hear all your voices. It would do me good to be scolded by Lucy and see Anna looking pretty and simple and sentimental. . . . No doubt you have whiskers now, and can look over my shoulder. You will call me your little brother. I feel the want of some of you in this strange land. I long for a home about me. When they told me many years ago that I had a double crown on my head, and that I should cross seas, it fired my imagination. I thought it would be simply glorious to get away from home, and roam in other lands. But how I wish I could see that home now. . . . The other day some one called me an old bachelor. It turned me quite sick. I went home and counted my years. When that crooked three gets at the wrong side of one's years, it loses its grace. Some one recently gave me a little book called *A Picture of New York*. It has a map in the beginning. I have been amusing myself in going through the streets with a pin, fancying I meet old friends and stop to speak to them; but that is in imagination only."

On May 8, 1823, his musical play named "Clari, The Maid of Milan" was produced at Covent Garden in London, England. In this play his composition, "Home, Sweet Home," was sung for the first time. While the play itself was not a great success, the song was very well received. "Clari" was produced in New York in November of the same year, and "Home, Sweet Home," quickly attained great popularity. It was sung in the streets and whistled everywhere. It brought enormous profits to the publishers, but, owing perhaps to carelessness on the part of the author, it brought him practically nothing.

For many years after the song was written, Payne had the strange experience of hearing it sung in homes as he passed along the streets, or listening to it being rendered by orchestras, yet he, the author of the masterpiece, had scarce enough to keep body and soul together. He returned to America practically penniless, and tried many projects, none of which seemed to prosper. He went as American consul to Tunis, returned to America, then accepted reappointment. He remained throughout life kindly, genial, and industrious, yet seemingly followed by misfortunes which dogged his footsteps almost to the end. He died at Tunis on April 10, 1852.

Thirty-one years later, in 1883, his coffin was disinterred and carried to the little Protestant church in Tunis, where the chancel window is inscribed with his name. As his remains were brought into the little building, an Englishman at the organ played softly the air of "Home, Sweet Home," while an American lady sang the song with deep feeling. The body was taken to

Marseilles, and there placed upon a steamer bound for New York, and in June, 1883, the remains were reinterred in Washington, D. C., while a vast throng joined in singing "Home, Sweet Home."

Will Carleton, writer of so many popular ballads, expressed what thousands felt in a delightful poem entitled "Coming Home at Last":

The banishment was overlong,
*   But it will soon be past;*
The man who wrote home's sweetest song
*   Is coming home at last!*
For years his poor abode was seen
*   In foreign lands alone*
And waves have thundered loud between
*   This singer and his own.*
But he will soon be journeying
*   To friends across the sea;*
And grander than of any king
*   His welcome here shall be.*

He wandered o'er the dreary earth,
*   Forgotten and alone;*
He who could teach home's matchless worth,
*   Ne'er had one of his own.*
'Neath winter's cloud and summer's sun,
*   Along the hilly road,*
He bore his great heart, and had none
*   To help him with his load;*

And wheresoever in his round
  He went with weary tread,
His sweet, pathetic song he found
  Had floated on ahead!

He heard the melodies it made
  Come pealing o'er and o'er,
From royal music bands that played
  Before the palace door;
He heard its gentle tones of love
  From many a cottage creep,
When tender mothers strove to sing
  Their little babes to sleep;
And wheresoe'er true love had birth,
  This thrilling song had flown;
But he who taught home's matchless worth
  Had no home of his own!

The banishment was overlong,
  But it will soon be past;
The man who wrote home's sweetest song
  Shall have a home at last!
And he shall rest where laurels wave
  And fragrant grasses twine;
His sweetly kept and honored grave
  Shall be a sacred shrine.
And pilgrims with glad eyes grown dim
  Will fondly bend above
The man who sung the triumph hymn
  Of earth's divinest love.

The Old Folks at Home
by Stephen Foster

'Way down upon de Swanee
    Ribber,
  Far, far away;
Dere's where my heart is
    turning ebber,
  Dere's where de old folks
    stay.
All up and down de whole
    creation,
  Sadly I roam,
Still longing for de old plan-
    tation,
  And for de old folks at
    home.

CHORUS

All de world am sad and dreary,
  Eb'rywhere I roam.
Oh, darkies, how my heart grows weary,
  Far from de old folks at home.

All round de little farm I wandered,
  When I was young;
Den many happy days I squandered,
  Many de songs I sung.
When I was playing with my brudder,
  Happy was I;
Oh, take me to my kind old mudder!
  Dere let me live and die.

One little hut among de bushes,
  One dat I love;
Still sadly to my mem'ry rushes,
  No matter where I rove.
When shall I see de bees a-humming
  All round de comb?
When shall I hear de banjo strumming
  Down in my good old home?

XIII

STEPHEN COLLINS FOSTER

THERE is still standing at the junction of Penn and Butler Streets in Pittsburgh, Pennsylvania, a cottage which was built over a century ago, and where Stephen Collins Foster was born on July 4, 1826. At that time Pittsburgh was a struggling frontier town which few thought would grow into the great industrial city of to-day. It is a significant thing that Stephen Foster was born on the day that John Adams and Thomas Jefferson died. He was the youngest of a family of seven.

As a boy he showed a remarkable aptitude for playing tunes on almost any instrument he could lay his hands on. His sister Eliza had a guitar, and a dozen times a day she had to rescue it from the would-be musician. One day Stephen went out with his mother, shopping. While she was engaged with the attendant, Stephen, who was only seven years old at the time, spied a "flageolet." He had never seen such an instrument before, but in a few minutes he had not only learned to blow it, a rather difficult thing even for a grown-up, but was actually playing fairly accurately the air, "Hail Columbia." The shopkeeper was so amazed at his performance that he checked Stephen's mother from giving him a scolding.

When he was fourteen years old Stephen was sent to school at Athens, Pennsylvania, where he did not distinguish himself by attention to studies, although he did attract attention and admiration from other pupils by his ability to play practically anything on the flute. This flute and he were inseparable, and he used to walk around the streets asking boys to whistle a tune, and though he had never heard the tune before, in a few minutes he could play it so well that he became the center of an admiring group. At this time he wrote his first musical composition—a flute waltz which called for four instruments. He was self-taught, not only as far as the flute was concerned, but in regard to several other instruments, including the piano.

In those days there was a great deal of community singing throughout the United States, and the Negro minstrel show was exceedingly popular. Christy, the originator of Christy's Minstrels, was perhaps one of the best known men of his day, and there were few small towns that could not boast a minstrel troupe. Prizes were offered for the best songs that could be rendered at these entertainments, and it was doubtless with the hope of securing an occasional prize that Stephen Foster began to write his songs which are now sung the world over.

His first songs were "Louisiana Belle"; "O Susanna"; "Uncle Ned"; "Away Down South"; and "Nellie was a Lady." These all, somewhat plaintive, tender, and sympathetic in their setting, became exceedingly popular. They were sung and whistled everywhere, and although Stephen Foster hardly knew what was happening, he soon became one of the most-talked-of men of his day. At thirteen years of age this marvelous boy wrote: "Sadly to Mine Heart Appealing" and three years later he composed "Open Thy Lattice, Love." His songs were his own in a double sense, because in nearly every case he wrote both words and music.

He followed up his early efforts by writing other songs, such as "Old Black Joe"; "Massa's in de Cold, Cold Ground"; "My Old Kentucky Home"; "The Old Folks at Home"; "Gentle Annie"; and "Come Where My Love Lies Dreaming." It is not too much to say that these songs have been probably the most extensively translated of any songs ever written. They have been sung by millions. Most famous of them all is "The Old Folks at Home." Soon after it was written by Stephen Foster, Christy, the famous minstrel, heard it and offered to purchase it. With that indifference which characterized all his business dealings, Foster was willing to make a present of it to the minstrel, but his brother Morrison intervened and insisted upon a payment of five hundred dollars for the copyright. Stephen Foster considered that a vast sum to secure for a song which had been hurriedly written and had gushed from his heart as water from a fountain, but when one remembers that this song has been sung in nearly every country in the world, it seems a very small amount indeed.

Travelers have heard it in tropical lands as well as amid the rigors of the frozen north. Music-lovers of practically every nation on earth have sung this tender refrain of a homesick Negro for his cabin by the river. The author, who was himself a very sympathetic and tender-hearted man, realized that there is a strain of melancholy not only in the Negro, but in every person, and it is due to this truth that the song owes its undying popularity.

The selection of the Swanee River was a good deal of an accident. Foster had never seen this stream, but he wanted a word with two syllables which was the name of a river in the south. After discarding four or five, the word Swanee appealed to him. Thus he made that river immortal.

In 1850 Stephen Collins married Jane McDowall, the daughter of a Pittsburgh doctor. His married life was not a happy one, and he was soon separated from his wife and daughter and lived the remainder of his life alone. There can be no question but that in spite of all his lovable qualities Stephen Foster was a dreamer and quite intemperate in his habits. Those who knew him best—and he formed many close friendships—have talked of his devotion to his mother, and also have borne witness to the fact that vulgarity and coarseness of mind were foreign to him. He was chivalrous wherever women were concerned, and throughout life sent all the money he could gather to support his wife and child. But he sought stimulation by the use of alcohol, and it spoiled what otherwise might have been a brilliant career.

In disposition he was shy to a painful degree, and because of this declined a great many invitations to take part in social functions. It was only when he was singing to his rich baritone voice, or playing over some plaintive air on the flute, that he seemed to forget himself.

After separation from his wife he moved to New York and made his home in a cheap lodging-house at 15 the Bowery. It was at this address that most of his world-famous songs were written. The story of his days in New York is a sordid one. He peddled his songs to theater managers and actors and in saloons. One who knew him at the time said that he had no overcoat even in cold weather, that his shoes had holes in them, and that when his friends, out of sympathy, gave him clothing he pawned it for small sums of money. He seems to have been almost indifferent to food, for a few apples or even hardy vegetables satisfied his wants.

Early on a winter morning in 1864 his most intimate friend, George Cooper, received word that Foster was dying at his lodging-house on the Bowery. He hurried there and found Foster lying with his throat cut and blood issuing from his forehead. He was suffering greatly. Here is how Cooper describes the scene: "Steve had wonderful big, brown eyes, and as he lay suffering with blood issuing from his wounds, he looked at me with an appeal I can never forget, and whispered, 'I am done for, George. Get me a drink.' Just then the doctor arrived and forbade it. He started to sew up the gash in Stephen's throat. We took him to the hospital. It was found he was also suffering from a bad burn on his thigh caused by the over-turning of a spirit lamp. Three days later Stephen Foster died."

It is supposed that in the darkness Foster was trying to find a water-pitcher, and he lost his footing and broke the pitcher, upon which he fell, inflicting the wounds on his head and throat. It was not until 1900 that Pittsburgh honored the memory of Stephen Foster. In that year a handsome bronze statue was erected in-side the gateway to Highland Park. Morretti, the sculptor, portrays Foster with pen and paper sitting down to write some immortal song, while beside him old Uncle Ned strums happily on the banjo.

Whatever his faults may have been, Stephen Foster will always be remembered as a man whose own tender heart enabled him to interpret the feelings of millions. His songs will last as long as love for home endures.

XIV

FRANCIS THOMPSON

ONE day in 1870 a boy named Francis Thompson traveled in a railway carriage with a number of other lads to Ushaw, a boarding-school near Durham in the north of England. He was a sensitive, timid boy of eleven, and one who was present that day ever remembered how quickly the other boys found this out. They teased and jostled him until the bag of jam tarts, which a fond mother had given him, was soon hopelessly squashed. The boy himself, always delicate, looked sick with worry and fear.

Francis Thompson was born at Preston in Lancashire on December 16, 1859. His father was a doctor in that town, and it was his wish that Francis should study for the Roman Catholic priesthood. The years he spent at Ushaw were not happy days for him, owing chiefly to his extreme sensitiveness. He was delicate, cared little for games, and was a good deal of a bookworm. He could not understand why other boys should want to tease and torment him. Naturally kind himself, without a trace of malice or cruelty in his disposition, he failed to under-

FRANCIS THOMPSON

stand the boys who danced around him with mocking laughter.

Francis succeeded only moderately well with his studies. He was careless and absent-minded, and after seven years at Ushaw College the president wrote to his parents that, in his judgment, their son was not fitted for the priesthood. At the close of the letter he said: "I hope that God will enable you to bear this disappointment. I quite agree with you that it is time that Francis should prepare for some career. If he can shake off a *natural indolence* which has always been an obstacle with him, he has ability to succeed in any vocation."

He was sent to a medical college in Manchester, where he remained for six years. He made a pretense of attending lectures and taking notes, but his heart was never in his work. He disliked his studies and learned as little as possible. Whenever his father asked him how he was getting along he evaded the question. Anyone less adapted to be a doctor it would be hard to imagine. He would slouch along the streets with a book of poems under his arm while his untied shoe-laces dragged along the pavement. Three times in succession he utterly failed in his examinations. About this time he became addicted to the use of opium, a habit which severely injured him in every way.

In November, 1885, Francis sold nearly all his books, together with what few medical instruments he possessed, and with a little extra help from his parents went to London, where he lived for the remainder of his life. When he arrived there all he owned in the world were a few books and his meager supply of clothing. It was the beginning of a bitter struggle against poverty and ill-health. He rarely wrote to his people.

In London he soon found his way to the Guildhall Library and other reading-rooms. He became more than ever careless about his appearance, and within a few months was almost in rags. Apart from taking opium, he was not a man of evil habits, indeed he was intensely religious, but he seemed utterly lacking in energy and ambition. Love of poetry had become a passion with him, and often he moved along London's crowded streets, seeing no one, his mind dwelling on some poetic subject.

He was soon spending his nights in common lodging-houses; occasionally he slept in arches or huddled on a bench by the Thames. If he had a few coppers he went to a lodging-house; if he had nothing, which was often the case, he slept on the Thames Embankment. He saw a great deal of wastrels and tramps and was quick to admire much in these outcasts of society. But vulgarity and obscenity of language or thought disgusted him and he saw much that made him heartsick. He established himself as a bootblack, but he was so harassed by the police ordering him to move on that he gave it up. He was glad to hold a horse's head for a few coppers. Sometimes he invested in matches that brought him a little interest on his money.

One night when he was cold and penniless he saw something bright in the gutter. He stooped, picked it up, and as there was no one to claim it, put it in his pocket, rejoicing in the thought that he had at least a bright halfpenny. He shuffled along, wondering what he could purchase with so small a sum, when he saw another bright coin glistening in the road. This coin was a golden sovereign, and he could hardly believe his senses. As he put it into his ragged clothes, he was half suspicious that it was a miracle.

But even that did not last long and soon he was homeless, friendless, and ill. Often he moved rapidly along the streets simply in order to keep his chilled blood in circulation. He felt that his senses of touch, sight, and hearing were dimmed, and his thoughts seemed to move in a circle. Often he was dazed either from the use of opium or from sheer weakness.

At this time he made the acquaintance of a Mr. McMaster, who showed him much kindness. One night as he shivered along the street this man asked him a question about his religious condition. Cold and hungry though he was, Francis Thompson resented the question. "Well, then," said Mr. McMaster, "if you won't let me save your soul, let me save your body." This was agreeable to Francis and he consented to help Mr. McMaster in his shoe store, for which he was to receive food, shelter, and a few shillings a week. This was a happy interlude in his sufferings, but Francis was incapable of helping very much and he left of his own accord, although he appreciated the kindness of Mr. McMaster.

For some time Francis had been timidly sending his poetry to magazines. He seldom had money for writing-paper and stamps, and doubtless the manuscript reached the editors soiled and torn. One day in February, 1887, he addressed a manuscript entitled "Paganism" to Mr. Wilfrid Meynell, editor of a magazine named *Merry England*. This man decided to accept the essay and a poem, and wrote to the address given him, but the letter came back to the editor from the "dead-letter office."

More than a year later Mr. Meynell received a letter from Francis Thompson, who had seen his poem in print. Again it was difficult to locate the poet, but a message was finally got to him. Mr. Meynell asked him to call at the office. He had formed a very high opinion of

Thompson's literary ability, and was anxious to meet him. Mr. Meynell's son—who later wrote the story of Thompson's life—thus describes what happened:

"The door opened, and a strange hand was thrust in. The door closed, but Thompson had not entered. Again it opened, again it shut. At the third attempt a waif of a man came in. No such figure had been looked for; more ragged and unkempt than the average beggar, with no shirt beneath his coat and bare feet in broken shoes, he found my father at a loss for words. . . . There was little to be done for him at that interview but the extraction of a promise to call again. He made none of the confidences of a man seeking sympathy and alms. He even refused the offer of a small weekly sum that would enable him to sleep in a bed and sit at a table."

This was but the beginning of Thompson's literary career. He had sunk so low in poverty that he had almost starved; physically he was shaken and battered, and Mr. Meynell persuaded him to be examined by a doctor. "He will not live," was the doctor's verdict. Francis was sent to a private hospital, and, contrary to all expectations, after a severe struggle he was able to shake himself completely from the opium habit. His mind became much clearer, and his poetry vastly improved.

Soon other poems by Francis Thompson appeared in various magazines, and then came his greatest poem, "The Hound of Heaven." Although not fully understood at first, and even attacked by many critics, this long poem was recognized as the work of a great poet. In a few years over fifty thousand copies of the poem had been sold, and quotations from it were heard everywhere.

The turn of Thompson's fortunes, in some ways at least, did not make a great deal of difference in his way of living. One who saw him frequently in those days wrote: "He was the poet of the broken wing . . . he weighed his words and would not hurt a fly. A stranger figure was not to be seen in all London. Gentle in looks, half-wild in externals, his face worn by pain, his hair and straggling beard neglected, he had yet the distinction and bearing of a scholar. A cleaner mind, a more courteous manner, were not to be found. . . . No money could keep him in a decent suit of clothes for very long. He carried around his shoulders a strange object—his fish-basket we called it—which he used as a receptacle for books which he took away for review."

Thompson's friends had noticed for some time his distressing cough and suspected the truth—he was a victim of tuberculosis. He felt weak and jaded, and the least exertion wearied him. His heart sank; he had a premonition that he could not live long. He was persuaded to enter a hospital. From there he wrote to a friend: "I am a helpless, water-logged and dismasted vessel, drifting without power to guide my own course, and equally far from port whichever way I turn my eyes."

He died in the hospital on the morning of November 13, 1907, watching right until the end, with grateful appreciation, those who ministered to his wants. All he left at his death was a tin box of refuse, a few unopened letters, a spirit-lamp without a wick, and a few pens that would not write. He collected practically nothing, and presents were acceptable only because they were an outward sign of kindliness. Not until after his death was the spiritual beauty of his poems recognized, except by a few. He was indifferent—perhaps too much so—to the things of this world, but he had riches of another kind. It is not too much to say that he ranks as one of the greatest poets of modern times.